FROM FROM

Also by Monica Youn

Barter
Ignatz
Blackacre

FROM FROM

poems

Monica Youn

Graywolf Press

This publication is made possible, in part, by the voters of Minnesota through a Minnesota State Arts Board Operating Support grant, thanks to a legislative appropriation from the arts and cultural heritage fund. Significant support has also been provided by the McKnight Foundation, the Lannan Foundation, the Amazon Literary Partnership, and other generous contributions from foundations, corporations, and individuals. To these organizations and individuals we offer our heartfelt thanks.

Published by Graywolf Press
212 Third Avenue North, Suite 485
Minneapolis, Minnesota 55401

www.graywolfpress.org

Published in the United States of America
Printed in Canada

ISBN 978-1-64445-221-9 (paperback)
ISBN 978-1-64445-222-6 (ebook)

2 4 6 8 9 7 5 3 1
First Graywolf Printing, 2023

Library of Congress Control Number: 2022938624

Cover design: Jeenee Lee

for Toby

CONTENTS

Is there a direction home that doesn't point backward?

—PAUL CHAN

FROM FROM

STUDY OF TWO FIGURES (PASIPHAË / SADO)

One figure is female, the other is male.

Both are contained.

One figure is mythical, the other historical.

They occupy different millennia, different continents.

But both figures are considered Asian—one from Colchis, one from Korea.

To mention the Asianness of the figures creates a "racial marker" in the poem.

This means that the poem can no longer pass as a White poem, that different people can be expected to read the poem, that they can be expected to read the poem in different ways.

To mention the Asianness of the figures is also to mention, by implication, the Asianness of the poet.

Revealing a racial marker in a poem is like revealing a gun in a story or like revealing a nipple in a dance.

After such a revelation, the poem is *about* race, the story is *about* the gun, the dance is *about* the body of the dancer—it is no longer considered a dance at all and is subject to regulation.

Topics that have this gravitational quality of *about*ness are known as "hot button" topics, such as race, violence, or sex.

"Hot button" is a marketing term, popularized by Walter Kiechel III, in a September 1978 issue of *Fortune* magazine.

The term suggests laboratory animals and refers to consumer desires that need to be slaked.

The term "hot button" implies not only the slaking of such desires but also a shock or punishment for having acted on those desires, a deterrent to further actions pursuing such desires, and by extension, a deterrent to desire itself.

Violence and sex are examples of desires and can be slaked, punished, and deterred.

Race is not usually considered an example of desire.

Both the female and the male figures are able to articulate their desires with an unusual degree of candor and specificity.

Both are responsible for many sexual deaths.

The male figure says, "When anger grips me, I cannot contain myself. Only after I kill something—a person, perhaps an animal, even a chicken—can I calm down. . . . I am sad that Your Majesty does not love me and terrified when you criticize me. All this turns to anger." "Your Majesty," here, refers to the king his father.

The female figure is never directly quoted, but Pseudo-Apollodorus writes that she casts a spell upon the king her husband so that when he has sex with another woman, he ejaculates wild creatures into the woman's vagina, thereby killing her. Although the punishment is enacted on the body of the woman, this punishment is meant to deter the king from slaking his desires.

Both figures are figures of excessive desire, requiring containment.

Both containers are wooden.

Both containers are camouflaged with a soft, yielding substance—one with grass, one with fur.

Both containers are ingenious solutions to seemingly intractable problems.

One problem is political. One problem is sexual.

They are both the same problem.

They have the same solution.

The male figure waits in the container for death to come. He waits for eight days. His son will live. This ensures the succession, the frictionless transfer of power.

The female figure waits in the container for the generation of a life. We do not know how long she waits. Her son will die, after waiting in his own wooden container. This ensures the succession, the frictionless transfer of power.

There are many artistic representations of both containers.

The male figure's container is blockish, unadorned, a household object of standard size and quotidian function. Tourists climb into it and pose for photos, post them online. The cramped position of their bodies generates a combination of horror and glee. This, in turn, creates discomfort, the recognition that horror and glee should not be combined, that such a combination is taboo.

The female figure's container is customized, lushly contoured. Its contours are excessively articulated to the same degree that her desire is excessively articulated. Artists depict the container in cutaway view, revealing the female figure within, awaiting the wild creature. The abject position of the female figure—on all fours, pressing her genitalia back against the hollow cow's genitalia—generates a combination of lust and revenge. This, in turn, creates discomfort—the recognition that lust and revenge should not be combined, that wild creatures and female figures should not be combined, that these combinations are taboo.

The tourist can climb into the rice chest. The tourist can pose for a photo in the rice chest. Then the tourist can climb out of the rice chest and walk away.

The artist can look into the hollow cow. The artist can render the contours of the hollow cow, the contours of the female figure. Then the artist can walk away.

Both containers allow the tourist and artist to touch the hot button, the taboo.

The desire and the discomfort remain contained.

Both containers allow the tourist and the artist to walk away.

The male and female figures remain contained.

Neither container—the rice chest, the hollow cow—appears to have any necessary connection to race.

To mention race where it is not necessary to mention race is taboo.

I have not mentioned the race of the tourist or the artist.

The tourist and the artist are allowed to pass for White.

The tourist and the artist are not contained.

I have already mentioned the race of the poet.

But to the extent that the poet is not contained, the poet is allowed to pass for White.

I have already mentioned the race of the male and female figures.

The male and female figures are contained.

The rice chest and the hollow cow are containers.

The rice chest and the hollow cow are not the only containers in this poem.

Colchis and Korea are containers in this poem.

Asianness is a container in this poem.

Race is a container in this poem.

Each of these containers contains desire and its satisfaction.

Each of these containers contains discomfort and deterrence.

Each of these containers contains a hot button, a taboo.

The tourist and the artist can enter each of these containers.

The tourist and the artist can touch the hot button and walk away.

Each of these containers separates the slaking of desire from the punishment of desire.

Each of these containers is an ingenious solution to a seemingly intractable problem.

They are the same problem.

They have the same solution.

Each of these containers ensures the frictionless transfer of power.

Each of these containers holds a male or female figure.

The name of the male figure can be translated as "Think of me in sadness."

The name of the female figure can be translated as "I shine for all of you."

I. ASIA MINOR

MARSYAS, AFTER

Dust loves me now, along with
leaflets, plastic bags, anything

unattached, anything looking
for somewhere to stop, something

to emblazon. Too painful
to brush them off, the day's

adhesions, too much
a reenactment. I float in my tub

of blood-warm water; element
of indecision, if only

it could be my habitat,
if only the sawtoothed air

didn't insist on its own
uninterrupted necessity.

I hate it, but lacking skin, I've lost
my capacity for scorn: that

was my failing—not excess
of pride, but that stooping

to pick up their accoutrements,
as if emulation could engender

equality. I stain everything
I touch, it all stains me;

my raw surface is an unlidded eye,
each stimulus its own white-

hot knife, but why would I
submit to be resheathed?

To lessen pain? What used
to distinguish me is already

defeated, limp trophy
flag of conquest; now I could be

like them if I chose.
But the acidulated

rain imposes a least
common denominator

democracy, it scours away
the pigments they used

to humanize their marmoreal self-
regard, their eyes gone dull

as the calluses I would suffer
forever rather than become.

STUDY OF TWO FIGURES (ORPHEUS / EURYDICE)

was it   that glance   backward
downward   so evidently   an afterthought

the body   performing   relentless
perpendicular   as if to say   this place

where   you abide   this is not
a place   I can abide   this is

a hell to me   the exit   trajectory
of the body   the declension   of the head

congruent   to tenderness   congruent
to condescension as if to say   you must

keep up   I will not   stay
the eyelids   half shuttered   the gaze

aslant   as if to say   askance
was it that   glancing   that angled

glance   that pinned   you to your
eventuality   your body this   extension

ladder   reaching up   to my unwalled
claim   o my irrevocable dawn

STUDY OF TWO FIGURES (ECHO / NARCISSUS)

after Carl Phillips

To "force a flower" sounds more violent
than the process turns out to be: more a sequence
of planned deprivations, fashioning a little well
of want—

        any "force," such as it is, inheres
in this excess of intentionality, the way one
might set a table or bait a trap. It's an American
tendency to treat such

            deliberateness, such
care, as itself proof of guilt—premeditation
as what tips the scales from mere mishap
into crime.

        Meanwhile the flower wakes,
as if alone, knowing no difference between
a natural or built environment, knowing only
its own desire, but not

          that there should be
something other than itself to desire: the water
it can dimly sense but never touch, on pain
of rot; the sun

        a theorized absence it mistakes
for purpose or for self, as if purpose and self
could even be differentiated at this early stage.
For the flower is childish,

               endlessly so, lacking
roots, lacking gratitude, its whole being one ever-
more pallid, evermore drawn-out throat,
as if trying to climb out of

               its own earthliness
through its single-minded focus on what
it wants. "I want / want I"—the mirror
that makes two

           out of one, the water
you maintain at a level just out of reach,
assiduously, because to gratify its desire
would be to spoil

            the innocence that is
the point of all your carefully calibrated
effort, the innocence you think enviable
in its centripetal

          self-regard, your
cultivation of an unslaked want that
reflects your own mirror-image wanting,
this denial that will end

             for only one
of you, in an outburst the color
of jealousy, star-shaped like triumph
or like the urge to hurt.

STUDY OF TWO FIGURES (MIDAS / MARIGOLD)

Everything he touches turns yellow.

We are meant to understand this as a form of death.

Death is a wish to improve one's surroundings.

Which is to say to be dissatisfied with one's surroundings is a form of death.

To be dissatisfied with one's child, to wish to improve one's child, is to wish its death.

Her death.

The dead child is unchanging, therefore beautiful.

Which is why we say that death is the father of beauty.

He created her.

Then he created her again.

His tears gild his gaze.

They harden as they hit the ground.

They are a tribute scattered at her perfected feet.

Unlike other forms of grief, they are durable, portable.

A currency, they can be exchanged for other beautiful or useful things.

His weighty head lifts, a sunflower at midmorning.

The air glitters with particulate light.

He takes a deep breath in.

Aspiration.

A nebula of gold stars swarms into his open mouth.

Gold spangles the moving darknesses of his blood, his lungs.

Even the rivers in this country pave their streets with gold.

STUDY OF TWO FIGURES (AGAVE / PENTHEUS)

AGAVE: Bacchae of Asia . . .
CHORUS: Tell us.
AGAVE: I bring this sprig, newly cut, from the mountain. The hunting was good.
CHORUS: We see you and welcome you, fellow reveler.
AGAVE: I caught it without traps or snares. It's a young cub, a mountain lion, as
         you can see.

—Euripides, *Bacchae* (Robin Robertson, trans.)

1.

Agave fell in love with the sun.

She spread open her smooth hard limbs on the rocks and waited.

She cleared her dusty throat *ahem*.

The sun kept staring west she stared at the back of his blond head.

The sky unblinking stared.

One day she stretched upward suddenly like a geyser.

She wanted to be a magnificent fountain for the sun with dripping catchbasins where he could slake his thirst.

He must be thirsty she thought he has to drink sometime.

She pulled moisture up from the ground.

There was very little moisture in the ground she had to pull hard so hard the veins bulged out on her forearms and neck.

She looked down at her body splayed out on the rocks below.

In her absence her limbs had sprouted little black thorns in self-defense.

The thorns all pointed inward toward the new hollow at her center.

It looked like a ravenous mouth or a set of concentric mouths.

She was trying too hard she realized.

She had climbed too far up it was not sustainable.

The sun kept marching west like a legionnaire.

OK she said *fine I'll have a son.*

2.

Agave had a son.

They took a curving knife and cut him out of her.

Her hollow center welled up with sweetness.

The sweetness fermented stickily in the sun.

A caterpillar drowned in it his dying flavored the sweetness with soluble wings.

Her son drank from the sweetness she named him Sorrow.

Um . . . why? people asked.

She said she was at first going to name him Sparrow eater of seeds but then she realized her seeds were poison.

People kept asking questions.

She said it was an Asian thing and then they stopped asking.

Sorrow found the Asian thing embarrassing.

Why does Grandpa have to dress like that? he asked about her immigrant father.

Respect your elders she told him.

I'll show them respect when they show me respect he said.

That's not how it works she said vaguely *Confucius.*

We're not that kind of Asian said Sorrow.

The scar where they had cut him from her healed into an ugly white lump.

It looked like a white mask soon he was wearing it all the time.

3.

Agave snuck into Sorrow's room to watch him sleep she hadn't since he was a baby.

Even while sleeping he wore the mask.

Under the mask the honeyed sweetness was leaking out of him.

The mask's eyeslits oozed amber tears they hardened into lenses.

His hair on the pillow a fan of tawny spikes

The rasp of his breath he was sanding a surface smooth.

The next morning he poured his coffee into his goldrimmed mouth his goldlensed eyes unblinking.

How can you see wearing that ugly thing? she asked.

I see things fine I just see them differently from how you see them he said.

Agave dropped an extra cube of sugar in her tea she stirred and stirred.

4.

Agave's nephew was in town she decided to visit her sisters.

She loved her sisters together they were aunties.

They made a splendid dinner for their nephew and afterward went dancing.

Their nephew was drunk all the time but at least he spent time with his aunties.

Agave poured herself some wine.

After her honey liquor the taste was savory sour.

She thought about the sun how he had gone west without her.

She thought about her son how his lost sweetness stained the sheets.

She poured herself some more wine.

Mama juice she called it the aunties laughed.

She started to sing a song.

The song was very beautiful it had a river in it and the moon and trees.

The aunties joined in the chorus it was loud like a lightning storm.

There was a pale face in the trees she thought it was the moon.

She looked closer.

It was fringed in yellow like sunbleached grasses.

Its cheeks rounded out like haunches ready to spring.

Its tongue flowed out of its desert mouth like a red river.

Lion! she yelled pointing.

The aunties yelled *Lion!* they all agreed.

II. DERACINATIONS

DERACINATIONS: EIGHT SONIGRAMS

1. STORY

Shhhh! her mother said. *Sit down.*
Next to me. Time to read.

The girl climbed up on the couch,
crossed her ankles. *Pay attention.*

A yellow book. The title character,
George, lived in Africa, a continent

that on her globe was colored red.
The leaves on the skinny trees

looked like reaching hands.
A pink-faced man dressed

in yellow from head to toe
spied on George from a distance,

coveted him for his own.
(This was wrong—the Bible said

not to covet thy neighbor. . . .
But maybe they weren't neighbors

because the man was American.)
The man set his straw hat down.

This was a trap! He sneaked away.
George coveted the hat,

tried it on for size. His head
wasn't as capacious

as the man's. The straw hat
obscured George's eyes.

All that he could see
was its dark interior,

a shaded cul-de-sac cross-
hatched in yellow (like the crayon

she used to draw her family's skin).
The man crammed him in a sack.

George was caught! Ensnared.
Now the man could order

George around, instruct
him to be good. "George was sad. . . ."

He was destined for the zoo
across the ocean. Once aboard,

he was untied. He said thank you.
He sat on a low stool, consented.

George climbed up on deck.
Seagulls soared in the white sky.

George stood on the rail, raised
his scrawny arms, and then—

[on the page, a long dash]
"oh, what happened! First this—"

[a vertical expanse of white
meant to suggest drawn-out

anticipation] "and then this!"
You had to shift your attention

from what was written
to what was drawn,

from verso to recto:
a monkey head-down

underwater. Not until you turned
the page did you know for sure

he didn't actually drown.
They saved him, of course!

The girl's forehead creased.
But Mama, I don't understand.

Why the white spaces, the dashes?
Wouldn't it have been easier

just to say, "George threw
himself into the sea?"

Her mother considered.
That's a good question, sweetie.

The white space requires
you to pause for a second,

to feel anxious, a little scared,
so that the moral of the story

can sink in: Don't be too curious!

2. EDUCATION

What's this C in Conduct?
Brandishing the report card,

her mother ranted, irate:
Your teachers expect

courtesy, not disrespect.
She started on her rote tirade:

thankless etcetera sacrifice
etcetera etcetera. The second-

grader, teary-eyed, cut in:
But Ma, it was just one incident.

This one boy teases me every day,
calls me "Chinese Eyes, Chink."

So at recess I used karate
on him, kicked him in the shins.

The mother frowned, scrutinized
her daughter's countenance.

And did you tell him that Chinese Eyes
are better than American Eyes?

The daughter stared for a second,
then shook her head, downcast.

The mother hesitated, then chose
to carry on. *And did you inform that idiot*

you're not Chinese, you're Korean?
—No, Ma, I didn't get a chance.

The mother turned back to the sink,
the dishes. *And don't talk*

like a know-nothing American kid:
it's not karate. It's tae kwon do.

3. CULTURE

Her mother coaxed her
to watch her VHS cassettes

of Korean soap operas. *Overseas,*
they're called K-Drama. This one's

a number-one hit in China!
A kitchen lady sought to ascend

to the rank of—*it's not easy*
to translate . . . royal physician,

I guess. It's an accurate account—
a historical success story:

You, too, can be a doctor!
Ornate hats denoted status in society.

Schemers accused innocents
of treason, concocted toxins,

spooned them down the throats
of stoic silk-clad maidens. *I'd rather*

watch Dallas. On the first day
of third grade, taking attendance,

Did you shoot J.R.? the teacher asked.
The girl, stunned, didn't answer.

Well isn't your last name "You . . . ing"?
She affected a redneck accent

that stretched the dipthong out.
The other students snickered.

Each Friday night, the nation
tuned to CBS, her family included.

During commercials, excited
chatter: *It can't be Sue Ellen!*

That's who they want you to suspect.
You have to think the way they think!

This era of family unity ended
when her brother, the scion,

flunked a pre-algebra test. Her stern
parents issued a draconian decree:

three hours of study on school nights,
TV only on Saturdays. (Upstairs

the kids had a portable set
for Saturday cartoons.) The rest

of the family, addicted, continued
their weekly ritual . . . until one night,

her mother stepped upstairs
with a plate of carrot sticks.

A screech! The portable TV set
flew down the stairwell, shattered—

a glittery corona on the parquet
like a 24 karat tiara. Adios,

Victoria Principal! Next season,
DALLAS jumped the shark.

The family shifted its attention
to a shiny new series—DYNASTY.

4. NURTURE

She would never have touched one,
played with one, had she known

their real name was *wood
lice*. The word *lice* was icky,

tarred by association, a taunt
like the unending chants of *Whorey*

Laurie addressed to the pale reticent
girl, who was, according to hearsay,

the class slut. She wasn't certain
what *slut* connoted, not for sure;

she didn't know the source
of the whispers, which crescendoed:

graffiti on Laurie's locker,
boys yanking up her skirt,

a lit M-80 firecracker snuck
into her lunch bag. The climax

occurred when some audacious
preteens orchestrated an anti-

abortion march in Laurie's yard,
early on a Saturday, when she

and her parents would be inside.
Laurie stopped wearing tartan kilts,

barrettes, started sporting thick
black eyeliner, scissored,

shoulder-baring t-shirts.
The cadre of sadists returned

to their lunch-period routine:
paying hard-up kids, Chicanos,

to eat live lizards. The going rate
was thirteen dollars. She shunned

the cafeteria, sustained herself on cherry
Coke, Snickers bars and nacho cheese

Doritos. After school, she snuck
past the bullies, trying to avoid notice.

School was tense. To de-stress,
she tended the *pillbugs* in her yard

(her name for the little critters).
Their segments connected

so cunningly, like the articulated
knee joint of an armored knight.

They'd curl up like lead shot
and couldn't be enticed to straighten out,

by a probing fingernail or stick.
She'd cup them in her hand

like a prescription. When done
playing, she'd relocate her darlings

to the jade plant in the crocheted
planter—their retirement

condominium, their *deluxe*
apartment in the sky, as shown

on THE JEFFERSONS. *Succulent*—
a satisfying word. It sounds

like what it is. She liked to think
of the pillbugs there, attached

to the toothsome underside
of a leaf, suckling like dark

little buds of need. Soothed,
she didn't notice the dessicated roots,

yawning mouthlessly for sustenance,
the colorless mound of carcasses,

chalky around the circumference,
at long last relaxed, uncurled.

5. SCIENCE

In Life Science, they studied
genetics, the experiments

of Gregor Mendel. He took anthers
from pea plants with green seeds,

rubbed them against the stamens
of yellow-seeded peas. This account

left her strangely aroused.
She surreptitiously brushed

the tip of her breast
through her brand-new training

brassiere. Her nipple went erect,
as if on cue. *The results were consistent;*

replicable. Each cross was yellow-seeded.
But in the next generation, twenty-five percent

bore green seeds. What's the reason?
Her hand shot up. *Anyone except*

Monica? No? She took stock. *Okay then.*
—The yellow seeds were a dominant trait.

—Yes, that's correct. The yellow seeds
were dominant. The same calculus

applies to human traits: hair and eyes.
Black and brown are dominant,

and blue- and green-colored eyes,
blond and red hair recessive.

If these two strains cross,
these recessive traits die out,

replaced in the next generation.
The teacher drew some squares

on the chalkboard. *Now, this handout*
is your homework. On these charts

retrace your family tree.
Go back four generations.

Then color in which of your ancestors
had blue, green, or brown eyes,

who had blond or red, brown
or black hair. There's a chance

you'll have to do some research
into your family's genetic history.

The bell rang. Her friend Annie
tapped her shoulder. *Holy shit,*

you totally lucked out!
This is going to take me hours,

calling my Nana, my great-aunts.
But you don't have to ask anyone,

you can color in the whole sheet,
the same answer all the way down:

black/brown, black/brown, black/brown.

6. EPICANTHIC

For the last time, Mom, the answer
is No. I'm not going to cut

up my face, let them scissor
my eyelids, chisel my chin.

I'm not going to put stickers
over my eyelids at night,

binder clips on my nose.
I'm not interested

in looking like Connie Chung!
She stomped out the door.

At school the next day,
Andy Dennis and Conner Scott,

two wannabe studs, cornered her
after Texas History. *Hey,*

Miss Ching Chong! Is your cunt
as squinty as your eyes?

I hear you Chinese chicks
have slanted twats!

She grabbed her knapsack,
rushed off to French class.

Back home that day, she shut
her bathroom door, squatted

on the toilet seat, a compact
mirror between her thighs.

A single hair—kinky, coarse—
gesticulated desperately,

the sole survivor
of some natural disaster.

She sighed, reached
for the tweezers, yanked it out.

7. CAUTION

Frisky, her canine sidekick,
(she'd named him when she was six),

had taken off again, seeing his chance
when she let him out to urinate,

tunneling under the cedar stakes
of the fence (as was his much-denounced

tendency) to make his social rounds
of the neighborhood. She sighed.

It was 10 p.m. on Saturday night,
her parents were at the Korean church

for choir practice, and, conscientious,
she couldn't let the dog run loose

all night (not since he, uncontrite,
had once returned with an unsigned

note duct-taped to his collar: *I'll shoot
this fucking dog if I see him in my yard!*).

Honestly, Frisky, though cute,
was a pain in the ass. Untrained,

he had the bad habit of chasing
mail carriers, acquaintances (once

he knocked a pregnant stranger
off her bike). Only Asians, for some reason,

were exempt from these attacks.
He thinks we all look alike! Racist!

they tittered. She knew, that night,
where Frisky was: the faux-Tudor estate

across the lake: the Carsons' residence.
She was in homeroom with their son, Trey.

The cool kids had handed around
flyers for a kegger at the Carsons'

that Saturday, advertising a set
by his band White Minority (Trey

was both lead guitar *and* lead singer).
Frisky, though half her size (and,

moreover, neutered) nonetheless
liked to sniff around the Carsons'

German shepherd, Bitch. (That
was her name. Ha ha.) She didn't

want to knock at the front door,
asking for her dog, endure the sneers,

awkward, avoiding eye contact,
while they searched the dog out.

She didn't want to crouch
down in front of them to attach

the leash—the scenario nauseated her.
Luckily, another course of action

occurred to her: she could row across
the lake in her family's canoe,

skulk across the yard unnoticed
till she located the truant,

return to her own home, unseen.
Nonetheless, she put on eyeshadow,

lip gloss, a cute (but not *too* cute)
top. Best to be inconspicuous,

she dissembled. (She cherished
a secret crush on Trey, unconfessed

even to herself.) Her trusty canoe cut
through the darkness—her destination

shining like a signal fire. She docked.
What the fucking fuck? A seminude

couple in an Adirondack chair
cussed her out, then carried on.

The amber floodlight scattered
citrines across a swath of dark grass.

The yellow brick road, she thought,
skirting it. *Friiiiiisky!* she hissed.

By the poolhouse the dog, serene
for once, luxuriated—an odalisque.

His tail smacked the concrete
like a slow clap. *You idiot,*

she scolded, snapped on
the leash, retraced her route.

Another curse from the now entirely
unclothed, interrupted inamorati,

but otherwise their surreptitious exit
passed undetected. Success!

Home by 10:30, well in advance
of her unsuspecting parents' return. Not

till Monday did she learn the sequence
of events later . . . much later . . . that night:

a dirty-blond teenaged girl with "issues,"
with clear indicators of "ideation"

(a new term-of-art to her)—that is,
according to the Carsons. A drunken

semiconscious round of Russian roulette
(usually, even at the hardest-core

gatherings, understood to be charade).
But this time, the game was both truth

and dare. "A tragic accident,"
the principal said, when she cut short

the morning's announcements.
Oh god, y'all! The girl confided

to her nerdy but upstanding cohort
(this wasn't technically inaccurate),

I was there that night! I was <u>there</u>!

8. CANON

An artsy chick, she dressed
herself in "ethnic" patterned

skirts, read Plath, Sexton.
She scoured the library stacks

for Asian poets, seeking
a racial exemplar, an icon.

The sole result of her research,
one anthology: Paper Cranes—

cherry trees, cheongsams,
celadon teacups: *Orientalist*

cliché, she snorted in disdain
(she had recently read Said . . .

or at least the introduction).
At her high school commencement,

she received the Agnes Starcross
Poetry Award—The American

Heritage Dictionary
and a hundred-dollar check.

Then off to college. *Write what
you know*, said her workshop instructor.

Here's some Seamus Heaney.
She tried writing about her dad,

her childhood, family dinners (instead
of *gim*, she wrote *nori*).

She studied critical race theory,
attended a sit-in to coerce

the university to teach Asian
American studies (the upshot:

no dice). She dated an initiate
of a college secret society,

then unearthed his cherished
stash of yellow-fever skinflicks

(NAKED ASIAN NAUGHTY HOTTIES
TAKE IT IN THE FACE!!!). *It's _erotica_,*

not just porno, he insisted
when she ditched his ass,

*What, it's not politically correct
to have a type?* In her postcolonialism

seminar, she was taught to distrust
the commodification industry,

attempts to package Asianness
for Western consumption.

*As an artist of color, always ask
yourself: Who is my audience?*

the prof cautioned. *Is this authentic
interiority? Am I self-othering?*

Her new suitor was studying
Lit (but premed!): ardent,

sincere. For the holiday season
(nondenominational),

he gifted her a signed edition
of THE BEST AMERICAN POETRY (1996)

(editor: Adrienne Rich).
Omigod, I adore her! Thanks!

In the introduction, Rich critiqued
the *legions of columnar*

poems in which the anecdote
of an ethnic parent or

grandparent is rehearsed
in a generic voice

and format, whatever
the cultural setting. She shut

the reader, cringing. A rush
of blood tinted her cheeks,

but (since she used self-tanner)
wasn't noticeable from the outside.

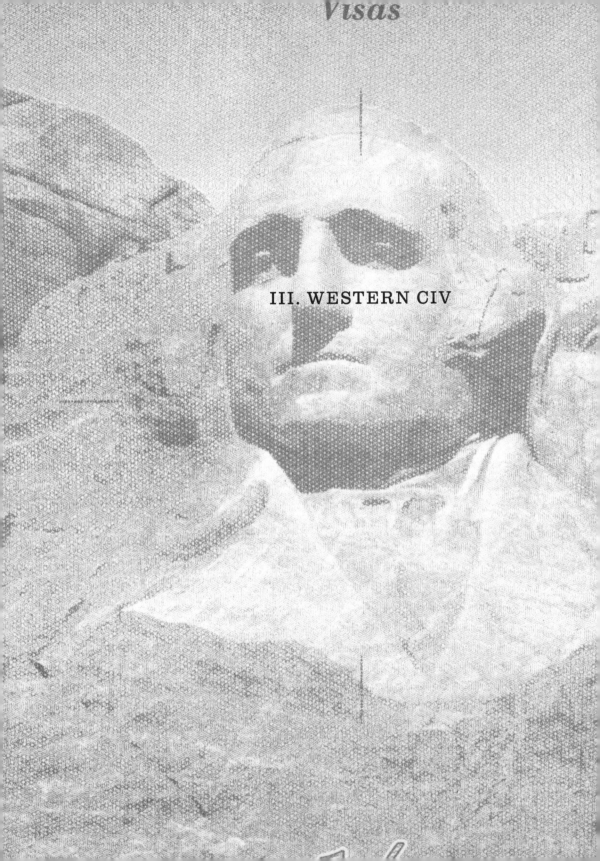

III. WESTERN CIV

INSTALLATION

Asad Raza, *Root sequence. Mother tongue* (2017)

In the forest a seedling cries for its rot-mother

A berry serenades a sparrow, a carcass sighs to its spores

Slow tremolo of fungi, the needle-whine of flies

The living stitched to the living stitched to the dead

The museum is a quarantine of cultivated silence

Our pale soliloquies coil in upon themselves, rootbound

Twenty-six characters, an alphabet no one speaks

The kindly curators import props to lend us meaning

The sun is a glass wall with gradients of gray and gold

Dawn is a rouged irrelevance to the east

We no longer worship the sky-dwelling pantheon

Each of us owns our own beam of magenta light

Each of us subsists on a cubic yard of Miracle-Gro

Nothing needs to die in order for us to eat

STUDY OF TWO FIGURES (IGNATZ / KRAZY)

You have written truth, you friends of the "shadows," yet be not harsh with "Krazy."
He is but a shadow himself, caught in the web of this mortal skein.
We call him "Cat,"
We call him "Crazy"
Yet is he neither.
At some time will he ride away to you, people of the twilight, his password will be the echoes of a vesper bell, his coach, a zephyr from the West.
Forgive him, for you will understand him no better than we who linger on this side of the pale.

—George Herriman, *Krazy Kat*, June 17, 1917

1.

The smaller figure is rendered as a grouping of ovals: head, torso, ears.

The roundness of the ovals suggests a kind of plenty—a trove that the line wraps around protectively like a mother's arm or like an electrified fence.

A circle is similarly bounded, but the radial symmetry of the circle suggests safety, stasis.

The oval, instead, is restless, pushing against its boundaries, seeking escape or release.

The line is necessary to contain the oval or to defend it.

The ovals of the figure evoke the pads of a prickly pear, tapering where they join together.

The prickly pear defends its precious hoard of water with its long straight spines.

The figure has no spines.

Instead of spines, the figure has sharp straight lines that make up its arms, legs, eyebrows.

The figure uses these lines to convey hostility—kicking, throwing things, expressing scorn or rage.

We understand these violent actions to be defensive, motivated by fear—a belief that the cherished contents of the ovals are somehow under threat.

But the ovals of the figure contain nothing.

Nothing, that is, except the underlying blankness of the page.

The lines of the figure separate the blankness inside the ovals from the blankness outside the ovals.

We are told to read the figure as white.

In order to read the figure as white we must read the blank background as white.

We have often been told that blankness means whiteness.

But this does not help us understand what it is that the figure fears.

2.

The larger figure is rendered as a continuous solid.

Most of the solid is filled in with closely spaced lines.

These lines are known as "hatching" or "hatchmarks."

We are told to read these hatching lines as blackness.

We are told to read the figure as black.

The figure has a white face.

I say "white face" although the face is blank because we are told to read these blank spaces as white.

The mouth and eyes are rendered as lines.

Were the hatching lines to cover the face, the expression of the eyes and mouth would no longer be legible.

In order for the expression to be legible, the face must remain white.

The hatching lines are pulled tightly back from the forehead like the wig of a founding father.

The exposed forehead, arching over each wide eye, suggests the possibility of enlightenment.

Enlightenment is rendered as a form of blankness, the unhatched space.

In order to achieve enlightenment, the hatching lines must be kept at bay like saplings rooted out to clear a field.

The hatching lines are "beyond the pale."

That is, the hatching lines are beyond the boundary line that separates what is clear from what is not clear.

We are told that the larger figure is also "beyond the pale."

We are told that the larger figure is drawn to the smaller figure.

We are told that the smaller figure is not drawn to the larger figure.

The smaller figure keeps the larger figure at bay.

If the figures were to encroach upon each other, the blank spaces would fill in with hatching lines.

These spaces would read as black spaces.

You would not be able to read the lines of arms or legs or features against this black background.

That is why they never touch each other because you wouldn't be able to read it.

STUDY OF TWO FIGURES (DR. SEUSS / CHRYSANTHEMUM-PEARL)

Unable to have any real children . . . Ted and Helen created a fictional one: Chrysanthemum-Pearl, born at about the time of Helen's surgery (hence her age was given as eighty-nine months, or a little more than seven years, in 1938), and a precocious child whom the Geisels could good-naturedly discuss at dinner parties when the conversation turned to children.

—Brian Jay Jones, *Becoming Dr. Seuss*

Each living Japanese is merely a link in this endless chain of ghosts.

—*Know Your Enemy: Japan* (original screenplay by Theodor Seuss Geisel 1945)

Infantograph

not a double portrait but one face inter-

polated out of two the mister super-

imposed upon the missus and vice

versa that is to say *super* as in extra

that is to say *impose* as in impolite

to force the real into the black-

box contraptions of the imaginary

for which there are many given

names and one of them is *hopefulness*

but not one of them is *father*

Pacific Coast

the marine layer like a swell

of flesh so cultivated so lush it

takes on a nacreous gleam the self-

soothing shield anxiety secretes

in self-defense to encase the incipient

irritant in a cocoon of quick-

dry sameness even the sun's gold-

tone strivings raise only the palest

painless blister after all what is a pearl

but a cyst sent to finishing school

Dream

in the doctor's dream the egg

doesn't hatch at once it bides it

abides it is bidden it bores a little

peephole it perceives it surveils it

extends a prehensile tendril

a periscope a peril it dispenses with

all pretense no longer tentative

it taps its tiny teletype machine

Flora

eucalyptus leaf litter gold love

locks scatter the doctor gathers

a fistful he fashions a gilt-

tiered coiffure (à la Shirley

Temple) whose filigreed

fretwork screens her secret

face *well-concealed* in Greek

(à la Trojan horse) translates

as *eucalyptus* a wispy whispering

gallery for Santa Ana's long-

winded insinuations *these invasive*

exotic imports outcompete

the native species their incendiary

seed capsules open only after fire

Dream

in the doctor's dream he sprints

from field to field he fits a lens cap

on the compound swiveling eye

of every sunflower in the drought-

dry orchards each almond's

peachfuzz hull splits in a sinister

slit he shakes the spawning trees

he speeds a combine harvester

up and down the teeming nut-

brown rows he feeds but there are only

so many he can possibly consume

Studio

in the window-walled room she is

practicing always practicing some-

thing is distracting her something

is scratching the inside of her face

her head down on the doctor's

slanted drafting table the doctor's

drafts slide toward her drifts of

avalanching failure ink-stained

flurries of bungled beasties she

shuffles them into single file their

arms akimbo ampersands linked

elbow-to-elbow a cancan line

of might-have-beens of kick-ball-

change their pointed toes like paper

planes they're dancing to the three-

beat cadence of her name *are you*

my real dad she asks the nearest then

the next-in-line the next-in-line

Beach

she's tacky with lipstick

kisses she's smeared

with unctuous brags

envious mutters cling to her

limp lace hankies charged

with static she flees

to the beach she scrubs herself

with saltwater with sand her

scouring only serves to polish

her to a serener sheen she

sheathes herself in a tawny

coat of camouflaging grit it

itches where her scratch can't

reach behind her face something

buzzes a bee that's lost its hive

Studio

The doctor is angry he wants to convince

America of those he thinks of as

America he surveys his ocean

view the sunset whets its billion

bayonets against the California

coast the native seaside cypresses so

decorative so sparsely spaced they

should be functional they should

interlace their roots into a living

wall a protective palisade to barricade

our sleeping beauty in her pacific

innocence he scowls he squints

his eyes he selects his inkiest pen

Dream

in the doctor's dream she

bakes his favorite chocolate-

frosted birthday cake he takes

a bite he spews a spray of kerosene

excelsior she lights the sparklers

the sun winks out the sky

rains chocolate bonbons paper

airplanes killer bees

Studio

she presses her buzzing

forehead against the picture

window she's killing time she's

counting off the little black barbs

of surfers that dot the waterline

their sped-up mini-pantomimes

of hubris *rise rise fall* she doodles

X's over the eyes of every cartoon

beastie every former friend every

day every month every year

Dream

in the doctor's dream the sunlight

fashions the facing windows into

mirrors a trapped bee ricochets

between them a maddened yellow

jacket a quantum of accelerating

light a pinpoint line too bright to see

the little light beam drills itself to be

a death ray practicing frustration by

frustration for its strategized escape

Studio

in the tower room she forces open

every window a whiff of Santa Ana

smoke wafts in a scatter

of desert scree a folded newspaper

flaps open like an overeager eagle

to show a cartoon regiment of slant-

eyed bucktoothed father figures

a chain of paper dolls ad infinitum

unreeling across the coastline

like a concertina queue with ink-

stained hands she rubs her own eyes

sees a daughter's face reflected she

dips a rag in turpentine she wipes

away the inky lines the milky shine

unbinds her coronet coiffure she

dissolves the buffering luster

down to her incessant itch a speck

of sallow grit flies toward the gold-

rimmed glaring eye of the Pacific

LEAVE

after Martha Collins

because it is to create an acute

angle an angle shaped like a

wedge because it is to give

birth to what you already know

to be expendable after it

has cleaned after it has fed

you because you are enriched

by even its deterioration because

the join might seem slender

like a throat because the bud might

seem tender like a bud but in this

tenderness you do not share you

do not share anything because even

the join is also a jamb a harbinger

of scab a rust-red portal that shuts

down what it depletes that shuts

out the obsolete because you keep

what is inside from seeping out

because you keep what is outside from

slipping in because in the singular

and as a noun you are a form

of formal permission as in why

don't you make like a tree and

IV. THE MAGPIES

PARABLE OF THE MAGPIE IN THE TRAP

A certain magpie was caught in a wire-mesh trap.

And the trap was small, and the magpie could not fly, neither could it stretch out its black wings.

And the trap held no food nor did it hold water, and the magpie was hungry and thirsty in the shadowless sun.

And then the hunter came, and the magpie said, Hunter, you should release me from this trap, for I am no food for you, and my meat is stringy and foul in the mouth.

But the hunter put food and water for the magpie in the trap, then the hunter went away.

And then the cold rains came and the wind, and the magpie huddled in the trap, and the magpie could not dry its feathers, nor was there any dry place for the magpie to rest its feet.

And the hunter returned, and the magpie said, Hunter, you should release me from this trap, for you cannot sell my feathers, for my black feathers are not beautiful, and neither are they proof against the wind and rain.

But the hunter placed a stick in the trap as a perch for the magpie, and placed a roof on the trap to shelter the magpie, and then the hunter went away.

And the trap was on the ground, and the coming night was near, and the predators began to wake in the shadow of the woods, and therefore the magpie was afraid.

And the hunter returned, and the magpie said, Hunter, you should release me from this trap, for I am no threat to you, nor do I prey upon your beasts, nor do I feed upon your gardens or your crops.

But the hunter placed a larger trap around the smaller trap and turned to go away.

And the magpie cried, Hunter, you must release me from this trap, for no animal preys on me, so therefore I am not bait for any quarry you might wish to trap and kill.

Now the hunter spoke, and said, Magpie, others will not come for you to eat you; others will come for you to attack you, and to drive you from their lands.

For know now, Magpie, that you are not bait because you are wanted, but you are bait because you are hated, and it is because you are hated that therefore you are valuable to me.

And the magpie cried and said, Hunter, what quarry is it that you take such pains to trap and kill?

And the hunter said, Magpies, and then the hunter went away.

PARABLE OF THE MAGPIE'S NAME

Pica pica

who was
it who

taught you
to want

what will
not feed

you that
you can

not make
a house

by eating
a wall

PARABLE OF THE MAGPIE AND THE MIRROR

A certain scientist had a cage, and took a magpie, and put the magpie in the cage.

And the scientist watched the magpie in the cage.

And after a time the scientist said, It is said that the magpie is the wisest of all birds. I will set a test for the magpie; and if the magpie pass the test, therefore will I know it is my equal.

The scientist took a tall mirror therefore, and placed the mirror in the cage.

And the scientist watched the magpie in the cage.

The magpie in the cage looked at the magpie in the mirror; the magpie in the mirror looked at the magpie in the cage.

And the scientist watched, and wondered, and said, How will I know whether the magpie in the cage sees that the magpie in the mirror is its own true self, rather than another identical magpie; for I cannot read the black lacquered eyes of the magpie, neither can I parse the jagged scribble of its voice.

Therefore will I mark the magpie and observe; if the magpie see the mark in the mirror, and if it remove the mark on its body, therefore shall I know the magpie knows its own true self, even as I know myself.

And the scientist took therefore the magpie, and placed a yellow sticker on the magpie's black neck, and placed the yellow sticker so the magpie could not see it except that the magpie see the yellow sticker on the magpie in the mirror.

And the scientist watched the magpie in the cage.

And the magpie in the cage looked at the magpie in the mirror, and the magpie in the cage reached up with its black claw, and tore off the yellow sticker, and crushed it in its claw, and let the sticker fall to the soiled newspaper at the bottom of the cage.

And now the magpie spoke and said, Scientist, I submitted when you placed me in the cage, and then I said this scientist therefore will know me as an equal.

And Scientist, I submitted when you placed a mirror in my cage, and then I said this scientist therefore will know me as an equal.

But now, Scientist, you have marked me with a yellow sticker, and to this marking I do not submit.

But because I do not submit, you know therefore that I know myself, and you know me therefore to be your equal, so now, Scientist, you must release me from this cage.

And the scientist said—not unkindly, for the scientist did not mean to be unkind— Not so, Magpie, for you have known yourself in the mirror, and you have seen yourself marked with the yellow sticker, and you have torn the yellow sticker from your neck.

And therefore you have passed the test by which I know you as an equal.

But because you are an equal, you must be marked with a yellow sticker in order to leave this cage.

THIRTEEN WAYS OF LOOKING AT A MAGPIE

One for sorrow,
Two for joy,
Three for a girl,
Four for a boy,
Five for silver,
Six for gold,
Seven for a secret never to be told.
Eight for a wish,
Nine for a kiss,
Ten a surprise you should be careful not to miss.
Eleven for health,
Twelve for wealth,
Thirteen beware it's the devil himself.

I.

"Mag" for Margaret, a chattering woman, a scold.

"Pied" as in parti-colored.

The offspring of a dove and a raven, not to be trusted.

The Pied Piper of Hamelin was brought in to take the rats but left with all the children.

"Pie" because you never know what's inside one; they'll eat anything, you know.

II.

Although magpies mate for life, a female magpie can "divorce" a male in favor of one who holds a larger territory.

So, upon meeting a single magpie, it's polite to say:

"Good morning, Mr. Magpie, and is your lady wife at home?"

Thus to suggest that even if the magpie has been rejected, at least this humiliation is not yet publicly known.

III.

In the Korean story, when the king told the lovers that they must be parted, exiling them to opposite ends of the sky, it was the magpies who volunteered to make a bridge of their bodies, once a year, so that the lovers could meet.

Did the lovers hesitate—not quite meeting the magpies' eyes—before accepting their offer, knowing that their black backs would make for treacherous footing in the night?

IV.

A magpie flies overhead, and for a second you see a police car, white doors open, dragging behind it the long shadow of the road.

V.

According to English superstition, if you encounter a single magpie, you should immediately spit three times over your shoulder to ward off bad luck.

But what kind of person holds at the ready such a mouthful of spit?

A store of liquid hunger that, by leaving the mouth, is instantly transmuted into contempt?

VI.

In another Korean story, the hero finally reaches the abandoned temple whose great bronze bell had tolled three times in the night to save his life.

Under the bell, the bloodied bodies of three magpies whose sacrifice the hero only at that moment deduces.

Again, the bodies of the selfless magpies had been put to another use for which they were ill-suited—in this case, a hammer, as before they had made a bridge.

Is that why the magpies have been teaching themselves to use tools, to keep from being the means to the end of yet another story?

VII.

They are not the same family, the various populations of magpies scattered across the continents.

For instance, the Australian so-called magpie is a type of butcher-bird.

All it has in common with other magpies is the name the English settlers gave it, white handprints on its shoulders and on the back of its black neck.

VIII.

In another superstition, the magpie's tongue is believed to hold a drop of the Devil's blood.

If their tongues were cut off, it is said, they would be capable of human speech.

In the cartoon series *Heckle and Jeckle: The Talking Magpies*, the magpies are visually indistinguishable, but one's accent is British, one's Brooklyn.

Each yellow face consists entirely of one wedge-shaped mouth.

IX.

The black and white of the magpie symbolizes heterosexual union as in the female / male balance of the yin yang.

Except in the Korean flag, the male yang principle is on top—that's what is meant by balance.

                X.

"Opportunistic" is the word used to describe the feeding habits of magpies.

Also certain kinds of infection that are not the original infection.

"Opportunity," which once meant coming into harbor.

                XI.

In *A Clockwork Orange*, the overture of *La gazza ladra* ("The Thieving Magpie") starts up to the sound of a woman screaming.

The camera pans down from a trompe l'oeil balustrade to the baroque proscenium of an abandoned theater, then to the woman being gang-raped on stage.

Cue "the old ultraviolence"—the jerky rhythm of the "in-out / in-out," the rise and fall of the sword cane.

For now it was lovely music that came to my aid . . ."

                XII.

As if the magpie were indeed as vampiric as the folklore would have it, using its dagger-beak to carve a bloody tunnel all the way through a larger beast.

A slander that led to the slaughter of 150,000 birds.

The way some bodies seem to attract slander, the see-through skin of the fallen chick disappears under a shimmering blanket of ants.

XIII.

And the most durable slander: the magpie as thief, bling-obsessed hoarder.

All scientific evidence to the contrary notwithstanding.

As if the cure for hatred could ever be knowledge, eyes lidlocked open, well irrigated, forced to see.

PARABLE OF THE MAGPIES IN THE WEST

And the magpies flew west and came to a land where there were many flocks and herds that were ill-tended and diseased.

And the magpies said to each other, Indeed this is the place we have been seeking and here we will make our home; for here there is food for us, consuming the vermin that so torment these animals and open raw wounds in their tormented flesh.

And this will be our work and the service that we offer to the Westerners; and therefore they will welcome us and reward us richly.

And the magpies tended to the herds; and therefore the magpies found their work and raised their children; and other magpies came to join them.

And the Westerners watched the magpies; and at first the Westerners were glad in their coming for the care that the magpies gave to those among them so long uncared for.

And therefore the magpies walked proudly among them; and the magpies had neat black coats and neat white shirts; and the magpies nodded their neat black heads and called to each other with loud voices.

And then some Westerners hated the magpies, and said to the others, See how the dark hands and dark mouths of the magpies are ever wet with the blood of their work and their food; surely therefore these magpies are unclean in their ways and therefore we should not suffer them among us.

And then a sickness came upon the land, and many died among the Westerners and also among the magpies, and those who were sick were cared for by the magpies.

And still some Westerners hated the magpies and said to the others, Surely this sickness came to our lands with the coming of the magpies; and surely therefore the magpies have brought this sickness to our lands through the uncleanness of their food and the uncleanness of their ways.

And then some Westerners hunted the magpies.

And some of the magpies cried out and said, Why do you hunt us, are we not those who care for you, even in this sickness?

But other magpies answered them, and said, But has it not always been so, you who have chosen to care for those who are not your own?

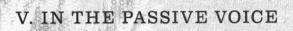

V. IN THE PASSIVE VOICE

IN THE PASSIVE VOICE

On the beach everyone hunches over, looking for sharks' teeth. Fossilized sharks' teeth wash up on this stretch of coastline—sharks shed them, the teeth sink down into the sediment, over millions of years turn to shiny black stone. They wash up at low tide, embed themselves in the scree. To find them, you can try to spot them as they wash up, snatch them before a wave pulls them back to sea.

The searchers are White, mostly elderly, mostly tanned to the point of extreme damage. Their red-brown blotchy backs broaden at their bending points like grass blades, presenting more surface area to the sun. Variegated, slow-moving humps, sea creatures as unnotable as the little brown birds darting toward then away from each wave.

My friend—another Asian woman—and I scorn the searchers. Their ungainliness, their skin damage, their irrationalities. "This is what happens when you introduce a commodity into a natural environment," I say, and my friend nods solemnly. But I'm wrong. The commodities were always there, are always here. Constituted as commodities as soon as a human observer showed up on the scene. We're hardwired to draw lines around pieces of experience. To package those pieces = quantization. To count the packages = quantification. If it weren't sharks' teeth it'd be egrets, Instagrammable sunsets, steps.

The ugliness of desire. Its bulging eyes, its avid rictus, its hunched and scrabbling abjection. This is why hunters wear camouflage, skulk in hides—to make themselves invisible, so that the only thing in the landscape is the object of desire. In first using the term "camouflage," in 1917, *Popular Science Monthly* described it as being "painted out of the landscape." Desire wants to disappear into its object. To be subsumed.

Desire abhors a vacuum even though desire is itself a vacuum, forming a stone out of the acids of its own churning emptiness. Desire hates itself.

In 1857, Jean-François Millet paints a picture of three women hunched over in a field, in the same pose as the sharks' teeth searchers. Umbers and ochres, faces shadowed, hair bonneted, bodies wrapped in aproned dresses, left hands behind their backs clutching scant handfuls of wheat stalks. Quantization. In the radiant distance, the white-bloused official harvesters bring in the ample harvest. The painting is monumental, as big as my dining table. Exhibited at the Paris Salon, *The Gleaners* draws public and critical scorn, hatred. "His three gleaners have gigantic pretensions; they pose as the Three Fates of Poverty . . . their ugliness and their grossness unrelieved," says Paul de Saint Victor, a noted critic.

I first see a reproduction of *The Gleaners* when I'm about thirteen. Our European vacation two-week bus tour stops at Millet's home in Barbizon. The mud-colored paintings don't impress my parents, who keep asking Rudy the tour guide—blond, Swiss, improbably pink-cheeked—why we didn't go to Giverny instead. I stare at the paintings with rapt intensity, make mini-moans, trying to impress Rudy with my connoisseurship, trying to differentiate myself from my parents. Later I tell my mom that when I make a million dollars, I'll buy her a Monet.

Quantification. I find four sharks' teeth on my morning beach walk. I walk 10,000 steps.

I first hear the word "gleaner" in Sunday school, the story of Ruth. Weird, I think. I prefer Arthurian knights and Greek myths. Ruth, the Moabite widow of an Israelite, leaves her native land and travels to Judah with her mother-in-law, Naomi. Ruth gleans barley from a harvested field and is spotted by Boaz, who owns the field. Boaz recognizes Ruth as the widow of a kinsman and tells his laborers to scatter extra grain in the field for his foreign relation to glean.

Why doesn't he just give her the grain instead of having it scattered on the ground for her to bend down and pick up? For her to stoop and scrabble, while he surveils her like a hunter in his blind? Why doesn't he just invite her over for a meal? Boaz sounds like a creep, scheming, leering—the long E's the soundtrack to a psychological thriller. What kind of person desires someone who is hungry, desperate, abject?

In 1920 someone takes a photo of a woman in the same pose as the sharks' teeth searchers, as the gleaners. On the bottom margin, an uneven typewriter has typed, "She gets 50¢ a day for cutting sugar." The photo is in my book *Korean Americans: A Concise History* (2019) by Edward T. Chang and Carol K. Park. The text beneath the photo tells me that the worker is in Hawaii, and the photo is courtesy of the Korean American Digital Archive, University of Southern California. No attribution either for its photo or its typed credit.

There's no indication of the woman's race in either the photo or its caption. I infer the woman's race from the photo's inclusion in this book. The woman's face is wrapped in a white cloth, under a broadbrimmed hat. Polka-dot blouse, an apron, a dress, men's trousers. I can't see her hands but her forearms are sheathed in white cloth against the sharp cane leaves. She's even more bent than Millet's gleaners, doubled over as if in sharp pain. Head down, hands busy.

Today, I get a message from my Brooklyn apartment building listserv. An Asian American woman says she was accosted by an anti-Asian harasser while fumbling with her key trying to enter the building. "This atrocious individual was spewing anti-Asian remarks and getting closer and closer to where I was." Our building is nearly half Asian, across the street from an SRO that's being converted into supportive housing—construction two years behind schedule. The woman signs off, "Ladies—you might want to get some pepper spray just in case." Another Asian American woman replies, "There are hateful racist nutbags out there right now. And the corner . . . seems to be more loitered with crazies than before . . ." I note her conflation of "littered" and "loitered," her conflation of homelessness, mental illness, and trash.

I draft an email in reply, urging residents not to call the police, who will only worsen the situation, who might prevent unhoused neighbors from accessing the nearby services they need. But I don't want to sound like I'm accusing this woman, preaching to her, at a moment when she's clearly fearful. I don't want to sound self-righteous, writing from a beach house in Florida, having spent six months of the pandemic at a cottage in upstate New York. And, to be honest, I, too, am fearful. During the pandemic, an Asian woman in Brooklyn had acid thrown in her face while taking out the trash. Another was set on fire. I never end up sending the draft.

Here in Florida, unlike in New York, you can buy pepper spray, have it delivered to your address. I order a two-pack, one for me, one for my babysitter.

US companies recruit Chinese laborers starting in the 1850s as a source of cheap labor, to work in plantations in Hawaii, to work in mines and build the railroads on the West Coast, to undercut the unionization efforts of White laborers. The founder of the Workingman's Party of California, Denis Kearney, writes in 1878:

> A bloated aristocracy has sent to China—the greatest and oldest despotism in the world—for a cheap working slave. It rakes the slums of Asia to find the meanest slave on earth—the Chinese coolie—and imports him here to meet the free American in the labor market, and still further widen the breach between the rich and the poor. . . . They are whipped curs, abject in docility, mean, contemptible and obedient in all things.

Dictionary.com lists three present-day definitions of *abject*:

1. utterly hopeless, miserable, humiliating, or wretched: *abject poverty.*
2. contemptible; despicable; base-spirited: *an abject coward.*
3. shamelessly servile; slavish.

To be poor is to be humiliated, hated, held in contempt. To be abject is to obey commands that should not be obeyed. To bend over, rump in the air, is an invitation to be kicked to the curb.

In the preceding paragraph, "to be humiliated, hated" and "to be kicked" are in the passive voice, a verb construction notorious for obscuring the subject of the verb—who is doing the humiliating, who is doing the hating, who is doing the kicking. "To be poor" is not in the passive voice because "poor" is not a verb.

During Reconstruction, Chinese laborers are also brought to the American South to undercut the wages and working conditions of emancipated Black workers. Congress passes the Chinese Exclusion Act in 1882, and Japanese and Korean laborers are brought to the US to undercut Chinese workers. The Japanese and Korean Exclusion League forms in 1905, and from 1907 to 1924, Congress passes a series of acts barring almost all Asian immigration until the 1960s. Signing the Oriental Exclusion Act of 1924, President Calvin Coolidge states, "America must remain American."

They are brought here for economic reasons, to make the poor poorer, to make the rich richer. They are brought here for racial reasons, to keep Black workers down, to keep Latinx workers down. "Are brought" is in the passive voice. The passive voice is used to be deliberately unclear, to be evasive or polite. "Is used" is in the passive voice. I am polite. I am evasive. I keep my head down.

Quantization. I take a walk on the beach. It's windy. No sharks' teeth, but tiny clams—rosy and translucent as baby fingernails—wash up with every wave. Within seconds, they upend themselves, burrow into the wet sand, rumps wagging desperately. A sandpiper swoops down, snatches one too slow to bury itself. A second sandpiper tries to steal the clam, fails, chases the first one for hundreds of feet down the beach, even though the beach is covered with thousands of identical wiggling clams.

In 1870, there are sixty-three thousand Asian Americans. In 1960, prior to the passage of the Immigration and Naturalization Act of 1965 (INA), there are nearly one million. In 2019 there are nearly twenty-three million, and this number is projected to double—to forty-six million by 2060. They are the fastest growing American demographic.

"Skilled employment" preferences in US immigration policy mean that many Asian immigrants are more highly educated than most people in their home countries, than the majority of the US population. Lacking wealth, they move into Black and Brown neighborhoods, into neighborhoods defined by redlining, by predatory lending, by past and present patterns of discrimination. They open businesses, obtaining leases, loans, and mortgages that their Black and Brown neighbors had been barred from obtaining.

In the previous two sections, I use the pronoun "they" rather than the pronoun "we." This reflects my discomfort with including myself in the "they." My family did not come here as laborers. Nor did they come here in the post-INA wave of immigrants, who—although many were highly educated in their home countries—often had to take low-paying, low-status jobs.

Through connections in the Korean government and the US military, my parents were able to emigrate to the US in the late 1950s, when Korea was suffering through the immediate aftermath of an American war. They attended college in the US, then graduate school, met each other, married, moved directly into the professional classes. Or, more accurately, they had never left the professional classes. Growing up in Houston, our neighborhood was otherwise all White. Our family's social circle was comprised of the families of pre-INA Korean American engineers with doctorates. All of them had gone to the same exclusive private high school in Seoul.

Flipping through my writing notebook, I come across a sentence in all caps, on a page by itself:

YOU ARE IN NO POSITION TO CRITICIZE ANYONE.

I have no memory of why I wrote that sentence down. Is it a self-admonition? A quote? I enter it into my search engine—just random tweets directed at Madison Cawthorn, at Ted Cruz.

Is it something I said? Is it something someone said to me? The "anyone" in the sentence feels like dissembling—it should be a "me," the sentence a strategy to deflect a perceived attack. To make the attacker redirect their punch so that their fist slams into their own other hand, cupped to receive it.

The sentence assumes that there are positions from which criticism is valid, and positions from which criticism is presumptively invalid. Is the stooped, scrabbling posture of abjection a position from which criticism is assumed to be valid? What about the position of the one who scatters the grain? Of the official harvesters, who might be objects of the gleaners' envy? Of the owners of the field? Of the buyers of the grain?

"Is assumed" is in the passive voice.

The book writes that Korean Americans were the "buffer between the affluent white and often poorer black and Latino communities." The book doesn't explain what it means by "buffer."

A buffer is "something that absorbs a blow, apparatus for deadening the concussion between a moving body and that against which it strikes."

As a term, "buffer" is another construction that leaves it unclear who is meant to be striking the blow—the Black and Brown against the White, or the White against the Black and Brown. Which is the "moving body"—Black and Brown upward mobility? Or White suppression? Korean Americans were not the buffer for the blow, they were the instrumentality of the blow, they were the blow itself, not the leather glove but the white-knuckled fist.

Everyone on the beach, whether walking or standing, keeps their eyes down, fixed on the sand at their feet. When the occasional person makes eye contact, I greet them loudly so everyone nearby will know I'm American, that I speak English exactly like an American. I am polite.

Buff is a beige color, deriving from the Latin word for buffalo. Buffalo hide is a light brownish yellow—hence "in the buff," suggesting both the color and the hide.

Buff leather was used for polishing—hence the verb "to buff."

Avoiding eye contact is one of the reasons Edward T. Chang and Carol K. Park give for tensions between the Black and Korean communities on the West Coast in the decades after the INA:

> [The Black community] believed that Korean Americans were purposefully disrespectful by not greeting them or looking them in the eye. Meanwhile, Korean business owners viewed their black clientele with suspicion. Koreans who had failed to assimilate into American culture continued to treat their customers the way they did in Korea, where they were taught not to look customers in the eyes or count out change because it was considered rude. The two communities clearly didn't understand each other.

Who is this passage trying to convince? Who could be naïve enough to believe this? That failure to make eye contact was the way Korean business owners manifested their disrespect of Black customers? Not by profiling them, not by following them through the aisles, not by crossing the street to avoid them, not by overcharging them, not by refusing to hire them, not by reaching for their purses, their wallets, their guns?

A buff can also be a blow—from the Old French *buffet*, meaning slap or punch.

"Rebuff"—meaning to reject or criticize sharply, to snub—derives from still another root, the Italian *buffare*, meaning gust or puff. To rebuff someone is to take the wind out of their sails. A buffet can knock the wind out of someone.

In describing the murder of Latasha Harlins, the book says that Du Soon Ja "accus[ed] Harlins of shoplifting a bottle of juice, which Harlins denied." The book omits that Du had pulled a gun on another Black teenaged girl several days before. The book omits that the store had a reputation for falsely accusing Black customers of shoplifting. The book omits that Harlins had money in her hand to pay for the juice, which cost $1.79. She had those two dollars in her hand when she died. The book says that "the two engaged in a scuffle, in which Du snatched Harlins' backpack and Harlins punched Du in the face." The book omits that before Du snatched Harlins's backpack, she called Harlins a bitch, grabbed her by the sweater. The book omits that Du threw a stool at Harlins after being punched. The book omits that Du's husband falsely reported the incident as an attempted holdup.

The book mentions that the news repeatedly showed the footage of Du shooting Harlins in the back of the head as Harlins was attempting to walk away, leaving the juice on the counter. But the book omits that Du was sentenced to no jail time for the murder, just a $500 fine plus funeral expenses and 400 hours of community service. The book omits that the judge in the case, Joyce Karlin, stated at the sentencing, "Did Mrs. Du react inappropriately? Absolutely. But was that reaction understandable? I think it was." The book omits that the LAPD largely abandoned Koreatown during the uprising, blocking off access to wealthy White neighborhoods and bottling up Black, Latinx, and Korean residents to vent their anger and fear on each other. I stop reading the book.

In April 2012, NPR's *All Things Considered* asks me to be that month's NewsPoet. You show up for the newsroom's 9 a.m. meeting, you listen as the team discusses what stories to feature in that day's broadcast. Then you have about two hours to write a poem based on that day's stories that you will read and discuss on the broadcast.

I'm lucky, I guess—it's a news day rich in tropes and images—the blind Chinese dissident Chen Guangcheng escaping from a house surrounded by twenty-four security guards, thieves posing as women in burqas robbing a Philadelphia bank, three hundred Priuses that had been purchased by the city of Miami found forgotten and rusting in a municipal parking garage. Quantification.

The first line I write is about Latasha Harlins, the story that April 2012 marks the twentieth anniversary of the L.A. uprising. But I write it thinking about Du Soon Ja. How much anti-Blackness Du Soon Ja must have eaten, drunk, breathed to have seen an honor student buying orange juice for her grandmother as a "threat to her life." Soon Ja is the name of my mother's best friend, who had lent me a diamond tiara for my wedding, a tiara she had bought in the eighties for her newborn son's future bride. (Turns out, he's a confirmed bachelor. Also, my own marriage recently ended.)

I think about Du's purported fear, how she must have fed it, nourished it, cherished hopes for it—that it would grow from inkling to actuality, that it would manifest, apotheosize. Fear as congruent to desire—both cut out a hole in the self then go questing for a shape that will fit that hole, fill it. Like the incomplete circle in *The Missing Piece*, rolling along, singing its song. I think of Du assessing each Black face, each Black body that walked into her store, searching for the shape that would make her fear whole. How she taught herself to crave the weight of fear thudding into the pit of her stomach like certainty. Like food.

I write the line, "Fear is the coin dropping into its slot." I'm sitting cross-legged on the floor in a windowless office. I have eighty minutes left. Quantification. I don't feel capable of being explicit, to figure out what I want to say, what I feel able to say about Latasha Harlins, about Du Soon Ja, about the LA uprising.

I pull up a rhyming dictionary on my phone and surround the line with a villanelle—a guaranteed crowdpleaser. It's a crap villanelle. I think I'll salvage the line about Latasha Harlins, that I'll write a more worthy poem about her when I have more time. That was almost nine years ago. It's been thirty years since her death, twice as long as she got to be alive.

Today a twenty-one-year-old White man kills six Asian American women and two other people at three Asian spas in the Atlanta area.

Also today they rename a playground in South Central LA after Latasha Harlins.

The Atlanta shooter, Robert Aaron Long, says he's not racist. That he wanted to "eliminate" "temptation."

Some White guys walk into a Korean restaurant in Atlanta, ask if they can get a massage, walk out laughing, high-fiving each other.

I walk outside, close my eyes, turn my face to the blazing sun. A clear red tide floods my vision, pours into me, filling all my hollownesses. I feel my muscles unknot, my hands unclench, my bones, my organs liquefy, becoming one substance. A free-flowing abundance I can barely recognize, barely put a name to. Rage. The Augean stables, the mounded-up, petrified shit of decades loosening, dissolving, floating away. An unending flow of righteousness welling up in my chest, a sulfurous spring, blood-warm. It stings a little now, I'm choking a little now, but soon I could learn to breathe in it. To inhabit it effortlessly as the red tide rises to swallow everything, a decorative froth on the surface like remembrance. Like poetry.

I walk on the beach. Everyone on the beach is White. I keep my head down. I find a clump of red, still-living coral washed up on the beach. I take it back to the house, wash it in a sinkful of fresh water, but it still smells of salt, of rot.

Today the FBI director Christopher Wray says "it does not appear that the motive was racially motivated." Even though a witness told a Korean newspaper that the shooter yelled, "I'm going to kill all Asians."

And it turns out that the Cherokee County sheriff's captain who has been speaking for the police department has been promoting anti-Chinese T-shirts on Facebook: "COVID 19 imported virus from Chy-na." I don't understand the misspelling of China. Understanding holds little interest for me.

I walk on the beach. A White man is surf fishing. I give him a wide berth. He's fiddling with his tackle. His fishing lure is printed with the face of another White man. He turns his back before I can recognize the face. Is it a compliment or an insult to have your face printed on a fishing lure? To be dangled?

"He was pretty much fed up and had been kind of at the end of his rope."

"Fed up" originally meant stuffed with food, "fed up to the back teeth." A British website quotes an 1832 court case in which a lawyer argued that the Duke of Bourbon could not have hanged himself since he was physically unable to stand on a chair and was also incapable of tying a knot.

Re: bloated aristocrats, the lawyer explained to the jury:

> Every thing being done for them, they never learn to do anything; they are fed up, as it were, in a stall to exist and not to act.

The Duke of Bourbon was fed up, in other words, so he couldn't have been at the end of a rope.

Robert Aaron Long was fed up, gorged with his supposed desire. The rope that kept him in his feeding stall he could have untied himself. But he claimed to be unable to untie the knot.

To destroy the supposed objects of his desire was not self-abnegation. Was not an exercise of willpower. Destruction is just a more wasteful, and therefore decadent, form of consumption.

Such luxury to anger, such waste, such laying waste.

My pepper spray arrives, in a box from Amazon Prime cushioned by plastic pillows like something precious. It's hot pink and looks like an aggressively sex-positive vibrator—the kind designed to ward off vestigial shame. To shame shame itself.

It has a key ring with a tiny fidgety quick-release mechanism, which I would be utterly incapable of operating in an actual emergency. The one time I was mugged, I couldn't muster the wherewithal to punch my attacker in the face, even though my right hand was free. I wonder if I would have a similar failure of nerve with the pepper spray.

I go outside to test the pepper spray. I face away from the sea breeze, aim for a pebble ten feet away. So satisfying—a needle-thin red-orange stream hits the target, seeming to sizzle, letting off a sharp, acidic odor. Like kimchi. Like anger. I am the Asian needle ant, I tell myself, almost capering. Invasive immigrant. Back away, racists.

Inside, out of the sunlight, my grin fades. There's the Amazon box to break down, recycle, the air cushions to pop. The Amazon logo is a curving arrow that supposedly resembles a smile but, because of the arrowhead, ends up looking crooked, like Jeff Bezos's smirk.

The *New York Times* prints a bar graph showing that as of 2018, 32 percent of Amazon's hourly laborers are White, 8 percent are Asian, and 60 percent are Black, Latinx or "Others" (Native Hawaiians, Native Americans, Alaskan Natives and multiracial). At the "Professional" level—i.e., lower-level managers—46 percent are White, 43 percent are Asian, and only 11 percent are Black, Latinx or "Others." At the "Executive" level, 74 percent are White, 19 percent are Asian, and only 7 percent are Black, Latinx or "Others."

The buffer in action—the light blue bar keeping the darker colored bars from encroaching on the pale gray, so that the gray can safely spread to occupy the upper tiers.

As a 2018 article in *Harvard Business Review* reports, Asians are overrepresented in the ranks of entry-level professionals. But Asians are the least likely racial group to be promoted, Asian women the least likely demographic to be promoted.

The buffer has to stay in place, above the Black and Brown, but below the White. Obedient. Docile. Abject. Rolls of plastic air pillows waiting to be machine-inflated, to cushion luxuries, to be popped.

There's a reply email from one of my students—I had emailed my Asian students to check in. She's from the Atlanta suburbs, and she tells me she's friends with the son of Kim Hyun Jung, one of the victims, that she's been trying to help him raise funds to support himself and his brother, now orphans. She's also worried about her parents, who are Chinese immigrants, frontline workers, unable to get a vaccine. I offer virtual hugs, an extension on her thesis deadline, which she is at first unwilling to accept.

Studies show that emails from Asian female students are the least likely to be answered by college professors.

I walk on the beach. There was a storm last night, which brings out the sharks' teeth searchers in swarms, in droves. White eyes on me. Back at the house, the tips of the red coral have gone gray.

The Atlanta shootings have given rise to a further surge of anti-Asian attacks. All the articles use the same word: "surge." A red tide. Many seem to be unhoused men attacking Asians collecting cans and bottles from the trash. The impoverished attacking the slightly less impoverished. But the daughter of late New York Senator Daniel Patrick Moynihan has also been caught on video, screaming, "Go back to China" at a young Asian American couple in Midtown Manhattan. She was identified because her face mask bore the logo of a performing arts theater in Woodstock, NY. The theater is named "The Colony."

There's a new viral video—a White man punches a seventy-five-year-old Asian woman, who fights back, beats him with a two-by-four. In the video, in the event's aftermath, the woman is yelling in Chinese, crying, her eye bleeding, pointing the board at her attacker. The attacker is on a stretcher, one hand handcuffed to the stretcher, the other partly elevated, fingers dangling. He has his head raised to stare at the victim, and, as she continues to yell, he tries to raise the purple middle finger of his sprained or broken hand, manages to raise it nearly halfway before the video cuts off.

My last day here. The coral is now entirely gray. It smells, simply, dead. I toss it, take one last photo of the beach and drive to the airport.

On the freeway, I'm going 80 mph in the fast lane. But a big white pickup truck flying American flags still cuts directly in front of me, brakes abruptly. I barely have time to slam on the brakes before it guns its engine, belching out a cloud of thick, gritty black smoke and speeds away. For a second, I have no visibility, I'm panicking, still going around 60 mph and unable to see the road, the median, other cars. I have my window open a crack and I'm desperately coughing, my eyes tearing up. He must have had his truck rigged to do that, must spend time cruising the freeways, looking for the chance to spew out hate.

Once at the airport, I do some quick research. Apparently there's a phenomenon called "rolling coal," where diesel-truck owners intentionally modify their trucks with a smoke switch to emit large clouds of sooty, particulate smoke—a retrofit that can cost as much as $5,000. These "coal rollers" are known to target hybrid and electric cars, protesters, and bicycles. But I was driving a nondescript standard rental. Was it because I'm Asian?

Back in Brooklyn, I resume my routine of taking my son to kindergarten in the mornings. Our city bus has new PSA signs: Stop Asian Hate. My son can read now—I hope he doesn't ask me what the signs are for. But I also hope he doesn't read the signs, internalize them, not ask me questions about them. He's already asked me why he doesn't get to be White like his best friend, like his father. I buy every age-appropriate book with Asian characters I can find. At our local bookstore today, there is one. I special order another two.

The next day we miss the bus, so we have to walk. We're already late, so I'm rushing as we pass an unhoused Black man sheltering under a construction shed. He's elderly, bearded. He spits, it lands at my sneakered feet. "Don't go outside," he mutters, his voice guttural. I cross the street, pulling my son by the arm, my heart loud in my ears. Did he mean to spit at us? Was his statement a warning? Because we're Asian? Or did I do something to invade his personal space, his boundaries? Or was the warning, the spitting, not about us at all? Does fear become a self-fulfilling prophecy?

"Fear is the coin dropping into its slot."

Six live caterpillars arrive in the mail—a present for my son's sixth birthday—in a plastic jar floored with feeding medium. The caterpillars start out minuscule, half an inch long, on a smooth rink the color and texture of clarified butter. Buff-colored. They take tiny, defined bites out of the medium, leave tiny beige poops like toasted couscous.

They barely move for the first few days. Then suddenly they've doubled in size, tripled in size, quadrupled—they're ten times their original length, revoltingly thick, bludgeonesque. A caterpillar will gain as much as 2,700 times its own weight—*The Very Hungry Caterpillar* indeed.

The poops aren't discretely defined anymore, they're not poops anymore, they're just shit. Shit smeared up the clear sides of the container, shit indistinguishable from the feeding medium, the whole bottom of the container a topography of caramelized shit through which the swollen caterpillars track their innumerable legs, twitch their eyeless foreparts, squeeze out even more shit. I move their container off the dining table.

The cover of the *New Yorker* this week shows an Asian mother holding her daughter by the hand on the subway platform. They're the only people visible. They're both masked, affectless, except that the mother has her wrist raised to show her watch. But she's not looking at her watch, she's looking sharply to the side, the entrance, as if she's heard something. Her daughter's head is turned sharply in the other direction, as if she, too, has heard something. A shadow covers the top half of the image like a scrim descending.

I haven't taken the subway since I've been home. Today I have to walk to a place two miles away. I could call a car service, but I refuse to spend my own money to avoid walking somewhere at 2 p.m. in my own goddamn neighborhood. But I take my pepper spray, clipped to the inside of my bag. Quick release.

About halfway there, a middle-aged Black guy falls into step beside me. "With me with you, you don't have to worry about anything," he says. He's jaunty, retro-styled. He has a beautiful voice, and I'm sure he knows it. "No one will mess with you." I roll my eyes at him, grinning under the mask.

When I get home, I check my phone. 9,741 steps.

All the caterpillars have climbed to the cheesecloth top of the container. They hang from their backsides, their foreparts curled up like an inverted clutch of candy canes. Their heads disappear first, merging with their front legs, fuzzy skin rippling, balding, shrinking to a taut gray-green with attractive gilt-tipped spikes. It's quick, a matter of minutes. The transformation pulses down their bodies, peristaltic, desire digesting itself.

Inside the chrysalis, the caterpillar is becoming an enzymatic goop with little discs floating in it like pasta in broth—discs for eyes, wings, legs—placeholders for eventual organs. As far as I know, by this point the chrysalises contain no actual limbs, nothing that resembles muscle. But somehow they're waggling frantically, revolving from their suspension points like gyroscopes in their final orbits.

The chrysalis is one-third the size of the caterpillar it had been just seconds before. Where did the rest of it go? No exit hole for shit. As if at the center of the chrysalis is a miniature void, a pinpoint black hole swallowing up the excesses of its past consumption.

In Ovid's *Metamorphoses*, Erisychthon, king of Thessaly, chops down an oak tree sacred to Ceres. The goddess curses him to be visited by Hunger. But not just ordinary hunger, "infinite, insatiable Hunger, / The agony of Hunger as a frenzy" (in Ted Hughes's version). No big-eyed poster children here, no winsome Ruth—Hunger, in the poem, is not merely pitiable but actively disgusting:

> Her lips a stretched hole of frayed leather
> Over bleeding teeth. Her skin
> So glossy and so thin
> You could see the internal organs through it.
> . . .
> And her knee joints were huge bulbs, ponderous, grotesque,
> On her spindly shanks.

Rather than emptiness, Ovid portrays Hunger as excess, as a failure of containment—mouth and gums failing to contain their teeth, skin failing to conceal its organs, flesh failing decently to cover its joints—the crude unmentionable mechanisms of the body obscenely on display. Abject.

The visitation of Hunger upon the sleeping king reads more like a rape than do most of the actual rapes in Ovid. Hunger

. . . bends above the pillow where his face

Snores with open mouth.
Her skeletal embrace goes around him.
Her shrunk mouth clamps over his mouth
And she breathes

Into every channel of his body
A hurricane of starvation.

But here, it is hunger—the most primal form of desire—that is the forced intruder into body and mind, hunger that carves out an unfillable hole in the body.

The king awakes, ravenous. Eats all his wealth, his entire domain. Erisychthon means "earth-tearer."

The king's daughter Mestra has, before the point at which Ovid begins this story, been raped by Neptune. Ovid apparently didn't consider this rape notable enough to warrant its own story. The aftermath of this rape makes Mestra a commodity: she can appeal to her rapist, Neptune; she can transform herself into various salable animals over and over again; she can sell herself over and over again, then return to her own form, return to her father. Over and over. Again and again.

In addition to being a blow, a buffet is also a sideboard, an object that offers up other objects to be consumed, an object that contains other objects deemed to be of value or use, etymology unknown.

Despite his lucrative exploitation of his daughter, the insatiable king can no longer forestall

     the inevitable.
   He began to savage his own limbs.
   And there, at a final feast, devoured himself.

As a kid, I tried to picture Erisychthon's last meal. Did he cut his limbs off piece by piece, or just bite into them while they were still attached? Was he ever able to get to his torso? His head?

I remember—perhaps a black-and-white illustration, perhaps just a picture in my mind—a lipless mouth hanging in the center of a forest clearing, a mouth that opens on nothingness. If this mouth swallowed something, into what void would it go?

If only Erisychthon had been able to evolve a mouth like a chrysalis, a mouth wide enough to engulf the body in its entirety, to digest the body into its entirety. Would that be the point at which even infinite hunger, infinite desire would reach satiety? The satiation of the self through the extinction of the self?

The very hungry caterpillar is an exemplar of desire. An object lesson. If desire is a hole in the self, the caterpillar eats and eats trying to fill that hole.

As if you could fill that hole.

But eventually it turns itself into that hole.

As if you could feed yourself to yourself.

Or maybe it's an exemplar of motherhood, as in that horrific book *The Giving Tree*, in which the tree feeds itself to the child, first for nourishment, then for profit. The neoliberal nurturer.

Postmetamorphosis the butterfly is posteating, posthunger. From being abject, subject to desire, it becomes beautiful, the object of desire. It drinks only nectar, the drink of the gods, unrolling its long proboscis to probe the flower with an avidity that reads as curiosity more than thirst, as if the butterfly were a philosopher deploying an unending inquiry.

The luna moth is even more a paragon of abstemiousness—it neither eats nor drinks. It has no mouth.

A pale-green ethereal wraith, it lives only to mate, lay eggs, and die. It's a sex machine.

I wish the Atlanta shooter had consumed himself, destroyed himself. Shot himself. Earth-tearer.

Desire can hate itself. I'm fine with that. But I'm not OK with desire hating its object. What he did doesn't deserve the name of desire. Doesn't even deserve the name of lust.

I have a broadside of a poem by Yusef Komunyakaa on my wall, titled "Lust." Its first line reads: "If only he could touch her."

My friend Anne Anlin Cheng writes, "Here's the thing that many people find hard to accept: Hatred does not preclude desire. Hatred legitimizes the violent expression of desire." She's right. I find this hard to accept. I'm still some sort of deluded romantic, I realize. I want to think of desire as exalting the object, not degrading the object.

DE + SIDERE = from the stars

But I realize this is just narcissism. If I have to be an object, I want to think of myself as a star. Celestial. Not as a hole. Not as the stuff that gets stuffed in the hole to be consumed, to be turned into shit, to be destroyed. Not as the buff-colored feeding medium.

Is there a model of desire that doesn't seek to consume, to destroy? A desire content to keep its distance, to venerate the hole in itself as a kind of shrine?

"I thought of walking round and round a space. / Utterly empty, utterly a source."

*

"Hi-dee-ho, here I go, / Lookin' for my missin' piece."

This evening I'm meeting a friend for dinner. Walking there, two blocks from my apartment, I pass a restaurant. It's popular, people crowd the outdoor tables. A White guy approaches me—he's in his thirties or forties, sandy beard, a hipster T-shirt. He's smiling. Are we friends?

He's not wearing a mask. He raises both hands, clasps them together, index fingers extended—a make-believe gun. He points it at me. *Pyoo! . . . Pyoo! . . . Pyoo! . . . Pyoo!* He's making little noises like a silenced gunshot. With each noise, he jerks the pretend gun upward slightly—a recoil—then reaims at me. He's taking his time, savoring each moment, luxuriating. I stop walking. He keeps pretend shooting. His smile widens. He's only a few feet away from me.

I look around. No one at the restaurant is paying attention. I think about flagging down a server, but I realize it's certainly not their job to intercede. I'm furious. I start yelling. "Fuck off, racist asshole!" I realize that now I'm the one causing the disturbance, screaming profanities, interrupting the restaurant patrons' dinners. I'm interjecting the word "racist," trying to get people to intervene. The guy is still pretend shooting. *Pyoo! Pyoo!* The restaurant customers are still ignoring us. I don't want to fumble in my bag for my phone, much less my pepper spray.

A Black guy pulls up on his bike, starts locking it up. He's extremely buff, wearing professional-looking cycling gear. I position myself next to him. "We don't want this racist shit in *our* neighborhood!" I yell. "Right?" I prompt the cyclist. "Um, yeah. . . . Right." He looks perplexed, conscripted into instant solidarity. I hope he doesn't think I'm crazy. "Get out of *our* neighborhood! No racist assholes here!" I yell at the White guy, who is still fake shooting, still grinning. *Pyoo! . . . Pyoo! . . . Pyoo!* We're at an impasse. At least the cyclist is still standing next to me. Everyone at the restaurant is still ignoring us. I thank the cyclist, flip off the racist, and storm away. I don't turn around to see if he's following me. I don't want to give him the satisfaction of seeing me afraid.

His eyes, the pinpoint voids in them. Avid, hungry for fear.

I don't want to feed him.

When I get to my intended restaurant, I'm hyperventilating from a kind of adrenalized *esprit d'escalier*. I walk right past my friend's table, who signals me, starts to tease me. "I was just assaulted!" I blurt out, then correct myself, not wanting to overstate what just happened. "I was just harassed. Excuse me," I say, and start calling the restaurant. I get an automated menu, have to hold for an operator. My adrenaline is ebbing. "There's a White guy outside your restaurant harassing Asian passersby." I can't believe I just used the correct plural of "passerby." The restaurant tells me they're aware of the situation, that he's been yelling racist crap all evening. Now I'm even more aggravated at the restaurant patrons. I give my number in case they need a witness, hang up.

Our server brings me a glass of prosecco, on the house.

My son can read now. We're reading *Frog and Toad Are Friends* together—he reads Frog and I read Toad. Tonight we read a story called "Cookies," which I remember from when I was a kid. Toad bakes some incredibly delicious cookies and brings a big bowl of them to Frog's house. In the illustrations, the cookies are tiny. Daisies loom over the house like trees. The frog-sized cookies must be the size of prescription pills, buff-colored. Quantization. I think they must taste like the Danish butter cookies my parents always had in the house growing up.

Frog and Toad can't stop eating them. After half the bowl is gone, Frog says they must stop eating or they'll be sick. But they keep eating. Then Frog says they need will power:

> "What is will power?" asked Toad.
> "Will power is trying hard not to do something that you really want to do," said Frog.
> "You mean like trying *not* to eat all of these cookies?" asked Toad.
> "Right," said Frog.

They don't have any will power. Frog tries putting the cookies in a box. He ties the box up with string. He puts the box up on a high shelf. But then he climbs a ladder, takes the box down, cuts the string, opens the box.

Frog takes the box outside, calls the birds to come and get the cookies. The birds come, take all the cookies, which are the size of crumbs in their huge beaks. Frog congratulates himself and Toad on having lots and lots of will power. Toad is sad there are no more cookies to eat. Dejected.

Rejected. Ejected.

Instead of being consumed, the cookies are destroyed. Does this make any difference to the cookies? The cookies are objects. If you're an object you don't get to object. You are in no position to criticize anyone.

Object. Subject.

But even if the cookies were the subject of the sentence, they would, by definition, still be subject to something else—is, by definition, under another's control or dominion, acted upon.

Project. Abject.

-JECT from IACERE, to throw, to impel.

A hand sliding from the shoulder to the waist. A hand on the back of the neck. A hand pulling on a buff leather glove.

I safety-pinned the cheesecloth with the chrysalises to the ceiling of a mesh pop-up enclosure, and today all six chrysalises hatched. The butterflies struggle out—wet, traumatized newborns—cling to the ceiling, drying their wings. I've given them a bouquet of wildflowers sprinkled with sugar water, some sliced tangerines. It'll be a few days before it's warm enough to release them outside.

The butterflies are orange and black, but not monarchs, to my son's disappointment. They're called Painted Ladies, like the priciest townhouses in San Francisco, like sex workers.

The butterflies ignore the flowers, head straight for the tangerines. They cluster on the sliced rounds, unrolling their long proboscises, stabbing them into the juice-filled cells. They look ridiculously cheery, as if toasting their good fortune.

Komunyakaa's poem "Lust" ends with the lines:

> He longs to be
> An orange, to feel fingernails
> Run a seam through him.

It's the culmination of a list of longings:

> He longs to be
>
> Words, juicy as passion fruit
> On her tongue.

and later:

> . . . to be as tender
> As meat imagined off
>
> The bluegill's pearlish
> Bones.

"To be" formulations, but not in the passive voice.

The figure wishes to be as tempting, as toothsome as fruit, as meat. He longs for his hunger to spark an answering hunger. Two voids that extinguish themselves while deepening themselves.

I read the poem again—it's the only version of desire that doesn't disgust me right now, that doesn't make my stomach clench up or make the spit run sour in my mouth. Maybe it's enough. For me. For now.

I ask my son whether he wants to keep the discarded chrysalises, which still hang from the ceiling of the enclosure. Buff-colored souvenirs of former incarnations.

I suggest he could put them in his "creature souvenir kit," which is an old metal lunchbox that holds some feathers, seashells, the tip of an antler, an unidentified animal pelvis we found on a walk. It also holds a little jewelry box containing the one hundred fossilized sharks' teeth I brought him from my trip. Quantification. He doesn't want the chrysalises, so I trash them, but I pull out the box.

The teeth aren't large, aren't sharp, but their black gleam draws the eye. They're little triangles, like mini dorsal fins. Millions of years ago, their owners were exemplars of hunger, what *Jaws* called "a perfect engine, an eating machine." Their circling became an emblem of fear, of a deliberate dance biding its time until the moment it churns into frenzy.

I pour all the sharks' teeth into my palm—they make a smooth, cool handful. On my daily beach walks I'd occasionally spot one, a tiny caltrop on which my gaze would snag. Then on the morning after the storm, they littered the beach by the thousands, a landscape in which miniature hazard signs were suddenly everywhere, unburied. The seagulls, the searchers, circling, circling

I clench my fist, feel the sharks' teeth grate together in my palm, circling, think about how many years it would take, how much pressure it would take before they ground down, indistinguishable from sand. But I don't really want to destroy them—things that are beautiful, things that I stooped for, things that I gave to my son.

They're not really teeth anymore. The organic material has been replaced by minerals, atom by atom, filling in the pattern of what had been. Emblems of hunger, of fear, transformed into objects of a small and easily satisfied desire.

"Fear is the coin dropping into its slot."

I pour them back into their box.

DETAIL OF THE RICE CHEST

In the 2015 Korean film *The Throne*, the rice chest sits in the center of the vast symmetrical courtyard of Changgyeonggung Palace

The film is called *The Throne* in English; in Korean it is called *Sado*.

A Korean-speaking audience would be presumed to know in advance who Prince Sado was.

An English-speaking audience is presumed not to have this knowledge.

Although this is a historical film, for a Korean-speaking audience, the well-known story functions as mythology, at the level of symbol.

For an English-speaking audience, the unknown story functions as narrative, at the level of plot.

There is an "I" in this poem.

I know who Prince Sado is, I can read the Hangul word *Sado*. But I do not speak Korean.

I am a member of the English-speaking audience.

I know about Prince Sado from *The Memoirs of Lady Hyegyeong* (1805). But I know about *The Memoirs of Lady Hyegyeong* from Margaret Drabble's *The Red Queen* (2004).

Margaret Drabble's *The Red Queen* is about Lady Hyegyeong. But Lady Hyegyeong was never a queen, nor is she associated with the color red. The name is misleading.

The name of the film *The Throne* is also misleading. The film does not focus on the throne, it focuses on the rice chest.

Like a magnifying glass, the stone courtyard focuses the gaze on the rice chest. The gaze increases in intensity and heat.

July temperatures in Seoul average 84 degrees Fahrenheit, with average humidity of 78 percent.

I have been to Seoul in July, I have worn hanbok on a summer day, but only once.

I have never seen a rice chest.

The rice chest is a functional object and stands in contrast to the highly decorative architecture of the palace courtyard. Its plainness renders it inscrutable, impenetrable.

Because of its oversize lid, the rice chest appears top-heavy, charged with kinetic potential. On its four small feet it seems to be crouching on its haunches, to be hunkering down.

"Hunker down" is a Scottish term that refers to squatting on the balls of one's feet, low to the ground but in readiness. It implies an apprehensive stasis, tense with the potential for sudden movement, poised to flee or to attack.

I have hunkered down, but only once.

Midway through the film, the rice chest is bound with thick rope, with a knotted webbing of four or five thicknesses of coarse, fibrous rope. The quantity of rope exceeds the function of the rope to such an extent that the rope binding seems decorative, symbolic.

I have been bound with rope, but only once.

There is something almost comic about such an excess of rope to bind a single imprisoned and dying man, the way there is something almost comic about a circle of guns pointed at a single unarmed man. I say almost comic rather than actually comic because, although these images provoke the same pent-up tension as suppressed laughter, I do not know who would find either of these images funny.

After it is bound, the lid of the rice chest is heaped with grass.

For a Korean-speaking audience, the grass-covered rice chest would resemble a traditional grassy burial mound, would evoke ancestral tombs, or even the prehistoric dolmens, which feature massive rocks perched on four small feet.

I have seen the grassy burial mounds of my ancestors, but only once.

For me, the rope-clad, grass-covered rice chest resembles a barbarian idol.

According to the *Online Etymology Dictionary*, the word "barbarian" comes originally from the Greek, meaning any non-Greek, and carries a derogatory connotation—those who speak a language different from one's own.

When I say "barbarian," it means I find the rice chest foreign, inscrutable, although it is Korean—Koreans speak a language different from my own.

In the film, the walls of the rice chest are made of thick planks, with chinks between them that admit slim shafts of light, drips of water.

But the walls of Korean rice chests are made of solid panels of wood. Planks with chinks between them would admit pests, especially insects, into the rice chest. Such a rice chest design would not be functional.

Partway through the film, we see a multilegged insect enter the rice chest through a chink between the boards.

The single insect is followed by a horde of identical multilegged insects wriggling through the chinks in the walls. We understand the insects to be a hallucination of the dying Prince Sado. Their function is symbolic, the danger of allowing chinks in the walls.

In the film, through the chinks in the walls, Prince Sado is able to see and to speak to his dog and to his ten-year-old son, the Grand Heir.

But, in fact, these incidents never took place. They are not hallucinations but fabrications of the filmmakers just as the multilegged insects, the chinks in the walls of the rice chest are fabrications of the filmmakers.

The chinks allow the gaze to penetrate what would otherwise be impenetrable, to penetrate the inscrutable, barbaric figure of the rice chest, to reach the human inside.

In *A Midsummer Night's Dream*, which is familiar to both Korean- and English-speaking audiences, Tom Snout, a "rude mechanical," plays the part of a wall that features "a crannied hole or chink."

The joke is that a human being portrays an inhuman object, since only an inhuman object would feature such a chink. I do not know who would find this joke funny.

When asked to "Show me thy chink," Tom Snout holds up two fingers.

I have seen boys hold up two fingers. Calling me a chink, they would place their two fingers at the corners of their eyes, stretching their eyes into narrow slits through which it must have been difficult to see. They found this joke funny.

I have seen men hold up two fingers. They would use their tongues to penetrate the chink between their fingers, rendering the gesture obscene. The tongue thrust between the fingers reads as sexual whereas an outthrust tongue without the fingers would be merely rude. Neither gesture is intended to be funny.

Both the boys and the men would use their two fingers to symbolize my body, a body that, without a chink, might seem impenetrable.

The primary meaning of the English word "chink" is a split or crack, a narrow fissure or valley.

"Chink" also has a racially derogatory meaning, referring to a Chinese person, or, by extension, to any East Asian person, since an English-speaking person using a racially derogatory term would not be expected to differentiate among East Asian people.

I have asked boys to differentiate among East Asian people. Upon being called a chink, I would say, "You're so stupid! I'm not a chink, I'm a gook!"

The Korean American comedian Margaret Cho later used a similar statement as a punchline to a joke. I find this joke funny, and some members of a Korean-speaking audience might find this joke funny. I do not know whether other members of an English-speaking audience would find this joke funny.

The term "gook" was used by English-speaking soldiers to refer to Korean people during the Korean War. It was later used by English-speaking soldiers to refer to Vietnamese people during the Vietnam War since English-speaking soldiers do not differentiate among East Asian people.

The term "gook" may derive from the Korean word for "American"—*miguk*. Hearing Korean people say this word, English-speaking soldiers thought the Korean people were calling themselves *gooks* ("me gook") and followed suit.

The word *miguk* in Korean literally means "beautiful country." *Miguk* is a transliteration of the Chinese characters *meiguo*, which also mean "beautiful country."

I know how to pronounce *miguk* but not *meiguo*.

There are several accounts of why *meiguo* came to mean "American." Some claim it's a simple phonetic approximation, others claim that *meiguo* was selected out of several possible phonetic approximations by nineteenth-century American missionaries and then made official in the 1901 Boxer Protocol after China's defeat by eight foreign nations. I do not know which account is true.

All commentators seem to agree that neither Korean people nor Chinese people literally believe that America is a beautiful country.

But both Korean people and Chinese people must call America beautiful in order to speak its name.

Neither Korean people nor Chinese people refer to themselves as gooks or chinks.

Neither Korean people nor Chinese people refer to themselves as Korean or Chinese.

Korea is an English word, which seems to derive from a mispronunciation of the name of the Goryeo Dynasty by Silk Road traders and was first recorded by Marco Polo.

China is an English word, which seems to derive from a mispronunciation of the name of the Qin Dynasty by Silk Road traders and was first recorded by Marco Polo.

I have said Marco Polo's name many times in a game that requires you to say his name many times. I do not know the origin of the game. Because of the R's and L's, "Marco Polo" would be a difficult name for Korean speakers to say, but I am not a Korean speaker.

I have called myself a gook many times.

I have called myself a chink only once, when a White high-school friend used the term in conversation, then stopped, realizing her gaffe. "Don't worry," I said. "I know what you mean. [X] is such an F.O.B." "What's an F.O.B.?" she asked. "Fresh off the boat," I said. "I may be a chink, but at least I'm not an F.O.B." We laughed together, to relieve the tension, although I do not think either of us found my joke funny.

I used the term "F.O.B." to show that I considered [X] to be foreign, a barbarian. I called myself a chink to make myself seem more American.

Fresh Off the Boat was my White husband's favorite television show during the time we were married. When we watched it, I hoped that laughing at the pushy Chinese immigrant mother on the show would lessen his dislike of my pushy Korean immigrant mother.

I hoped that allowing my White husband to treat my parents as endearingly foreign, fresh off the boat, like the endearingly foreign TV family of *Fresh Off the Boat*, would make myself seem more American.

None of the actors in *Fresh Off the Boat* are fresh off the boat. Nearly all of them were born in America. By pretending to be foreign, they make English-speaking audiences feel more American.

My parents are not fresh off the boat. They have been in America for more than fifty years. They speak both Korean and English.

A television is a box that allows us to put people inside it.

The television is sometimes called an "idiot box" from the Greek for "private person," from *idios*, meaning "one's own." But those inside the box have no privacy.

We put the inscrutable into a box so they may be scrutinized.

I made [X] inscrutable. I put [X] into the box.

I made my parents inscrutable. I put my parents into the box.

I decorated the box so it seemed foreign, barbaric. I made the box inscrutable so it seemed like a distant ancestor, I buried it so it seemed like a grave.

I made a chink in the box that the gaze could penetrate.

I stayed outside the box. I treated what was inside the box as a joke.

I was the English-speaking audience.

I watched *Fresh Off the Boat* on the idiot box.

I watched *The Throne* on the idiot box.

In *The Throne*, a parent puts his son in the rice chest.

After the son's death, the rice chest is forced open.

After the son's death, his mouth is forced open. Three spoonfuls of rice are forced into his mouth, rice that might have kept him from starving to death in the rice chest.

After the son's death, a name is forced into his mouth.

The name is Sado, a name which has meaning for Korean-speaking audiences.

I have said Sado's name many times.

The son never called himself Sado.

There was never a chink in the rice chest.

No one could see into the rice chest.

There is a "you" in this poem.

You are a member of the English-speaking audience.

I let you see into the box, into what is private, into what is foreign, into what is inscrutable, into what has been buried.

I am the chink in the box.

NOTES

Study of Two Figures (Pasiphaë / Sado): In Greek mythology, Pasiphaë is the wife of King Minos of Crete. She is one of a group of sorceresses and tragic heroines known as the Daughters of the Sun—descendants of the Sun God Helios— and her family members include Circe, Phaedra, and Medea. Her family is from Colchis, a region of present-day Turkey, which according to legend was fabulously wealthy. According to the myth, a white bull appeared among Minos's herds. Minos was supposed to sacrifice the bull to Poseidon, but instead kept the bull for himself. In punishment, Poseidon cursed Pasiphaë to lust after the bull. She asked the inventor Daedalus for help, and he created a hollow wooden cow covered with cowhide. Concealed within the wooden cow, Pasiphaë mated with the bull and gave birth to the Minotaur, a monster half-man, half-bull. The Minotaur was imprisoned in the Labyrinth, which was also invented by Daedalus, and was eventually killed by the Athenian hero Theseus. A number of canonical writers including Euripides, Ovid, Virgil, and Dante have written about Pasiphaë as a figure of unnatural lust.

Yi Seon (이선), aka Sado (사도) (1735–1762) was crown prince of Korea under King Yeongjo (영조), and his story is recounted in the memoirs of his wife Lady Hyegyeong (혜경). At age fifteen, he became regent, but was subject to frequent public chastisement by his father. He began to have hallucinations, developed a clothing phobia, and started to rape and kill palace staff to release his emotions. At one point, he attempted to sneak into the upper palace, where the king resided, in order to attack a court official. Finally, fearing for the safety of her family, Sado's mother asked the king to deal with the situation. According to protocol, the body of a member of the royal family could not be defiled. Additionally, if Sado were executed as a criminal, his wife and son (the only direct royal male heir) would also be subject to death or banishment, creating a crisis for the succession. To resolve this dilemma, in July 1762, the king ordered Sado to climb into a wooden rice chest approximately four feet square. Sado begged for his life before getting into the chest. After two days, the king ordered the chest to be bound with rope, and for grass to be strewn on top. On the evening of the seventh day, Sado stopped responding from inside the chest, and on the eighth day the chest was opened and he was pronounced dead. Fifteen days after his death, the king reinstated him as crown prince and gave him the posthumous name Sado, which translates as "to think of with great sorrow." A number of Korean films and television series have treated the history of Crown Prince Sado.

Asia Minor: The word "Asia" was originally a Greek word, for "land of the sunrise." The ancient Greeks generally used the term Asia to refer to Asia Minor, or Anatolia, which is in present-day Turkey, and surrounding regions in which the Greeks had established colonies, including parts of present-day Syria, Lebanon, Iraq, Iran, Egypt, Armenia, Azerbaijan, and Georgia.

Marsyas, After: In Greek mythology, Marsyas was a satyr from Phrygia, in present-day Turkey. In the myth, the goddess Athena invented a double-reed instrument known as the aulos but discarded it upon seeing that playing it puffed up her cheeks. Marsyas picked up the aulos and became an expert player, eventually challenging Apollo, the Greek god of music, to a music contest, judged by the Muses. After Marsyas lost the contest, Apollo had him flayed alive as a punishment, then nailed the hide to a pine tree. Scholars have treated the myth as a symbol of the supremacy of the Greek pantheon over the indigenous worship of Kybele in Asia Minor. In ancient Rome, Marsyas became a symbol of parrhesia, or speaking truth to power, and was associated with popular uprising.

Study of Two Figures (Orpheus / Eurydice): In Greek mythology, Eurydice was the wife of the musician, Orpheus. On their wedding day, Eurydice was bitten by a viper and died instantly. Orpheus traveled to the underworld and played and sang for Hades and Persephone, the king and queen of the dead. Moved, they agreed to return Eurydice to life, on the condition that Orpheus must walk in front of her and not look back until they had reached the living world. On the walk back, he began to doubt that she was behind him, and just before he reached the exit, he turned around, and Eurydice was forced to return to the underworld.

Study of Two Figures (Echo / Narcissus): In Greek mythology, Narcissus was a hunter known for his beauty. Rejecting all lovers, he eventually saw his own reflection in a pool and fell in love with it, staring at it and eventually wasting away. The narcissus flower—specifically *Narcissus poeticus*, which is white with a yellow center—sprang from his dead body. The introduction of the nymph Echo to the myth seems to have been an invention of the Roman poet Ovid. Echo was a "talkative nymph," who fell afoul of Juno by misleading her about Jupiter's whereabouts. Juno cursed her to be unable to say anything on her own, only to repeat what had been said to her. Echo fell in love with Narcissus, who scorned her love. After his death, she, too, wasted away, leaving nothing but her voice. The poem also references the process of forcing bulbs—including narcissus bulbs—which are induced to bloom by suspending the bulb above a water source. Narcissus plants are toxic to animals, other plants, and the surrounding soil.

Study of Two Figures (Midas / Marigold): In Greek mythology, Midas was king of Phrygia, in present-day Turkey. Dionysus, the god of wine, granted Midas a wish. Midas asked that whatever he touched be turned to gold. At first Midas rejoiced in his new wealth, but soon, of course, he realized that his new power prevented him from eating and drinking. In Nathaniel Hawthorne's version of the story, Midas's daughter—whom Hawthorne names "Marigold"—came to him, upset that her rose garden had turned to gold, and when Midas reached out to comfort her, she became a golden statue. Midas prayed to Dionysus, begging to reverse his wish, and Dionysus advised Midas to wash in the river Pactolus. Midas washed away the curse, and restored his daughter, and the sands of the river turned golden.

Study of Two Figures (Agave / Pentheus): *The Bacchae*, which Edward Said describes as "perhaps the most Asiatic of all the Attic dramas," focuses on the ruling family of Thebes. Cadmus, the founder of Thebes and the grandfather of the family, is described as "Cadmus of Sidon," in present-day Lebanon. Agave is his daughter, the sister of Autonoë, Ino, and Semele, who is the mother of Dionysus. Semele's sisters, including Agave, deny the god's divinity. Euripides refers to Dionysus throughout the play as "the Asian god," and refers to his homeland as Phrygia and to his followers the maenads as "Asian Bacchae." Pentheus, the son of Agave, is the ruler of Thebes, and tries to outlaw the worship of Dionysus. Dionysus drives the women of Thebes, including Pentheus's mother and aunts, into an ecstatic frenzy, and they join the maenads. Pentheus tries to arrest the leader of the worshippers, Dionysus, disguised as a "foreigner." Dionysus frees himself and convinces Pentheus to disguise himself as a female maenad and to spy on the worshippers. Disguised, Pentheus climbs up a tree, but Dionysus reveals Pentheus's location to the maenads, who tear him to pieces, led by Agave. Agave arrives back in Thebes, carrying her son's head, which she believes to be that of a mountain lion. Cadmus makes her recognize that she has killed her son. Agave and her sisters are sent into exile, and Cadmus and his wife are turned into snakes.

I'm indebted to Brooklyn Academy of Music for asking me to give a talk to introduce SITI Company's 2018 production of Euripides's *The Bacchae*. I'm also indebted to the Lannan Foundation, Marfa, where the agave plants in the surrounding desert influenced this poem, which references both the plant and the process for making tequila.

Deracinations: Eight Sonigrams: A "sonigram" is a form I devised that is similar to an anagram, but generative rather than constraining. A sonigram is a poem in which the letters and sounds of the original word are omnipresent, but the poem is not limited to those letters and sounds. The intent is to inhabit the sonic landscape of a particular word—in this case, the unobtrusive, nearly ubiquitous sounds of *deracination*.

Installation was commissioned by Jeff Dolven for a performance in conjunction with Asad Raza's installation *Root sequence. Mother tongue* at the 2017 Whitney Biennial. The commission was to write a sonnet in modular lines that could be read in any order.

Study of Two Figures (Ignatz / Krazy) was inspired by Michael Tisserand's 2016 book *Krazy: George Herriman, A Life in Black and White*, which recounted the *Krazy Kat* cartoonist's life as a mixed-race artist passing for White.

Study of Two Figures (Dr. Seuss / Chrysanthemum-Pearl): Starting in 1941, Theodor Geisel, aka "Dr. Seuss," became a political cartoonist for *PM* magazine. For the next two years, he created hundreds of political cartoons, many of which contained viciously racist depictions of Japanese people, and which suggested that Japanese Americans were traitorous. During this time, he also worked in the film department of the US Army, where he contributed to the draft screenplay for the propaganda film *Know Your Enemy: Japan*, which depicted the Japanese people as "as much alike as photographic prints off the same negative," and "an obedient mass with but a single mind." The film stated that "defeating this nation is as necessary as shooting down a mad dog in your neighborhood."

During much the same time period, Theodor and his wife Helen Geisel were unable to conceive a child, a source of much personal sorrow, as reflected in the children's book *Horton Hatches the Egg* (1940). Additionally, in 1939, Geisel patented a device called the Infantograph, which would attempt to show couples what their children would look like by combining photos of their faces. Starting in the late 1930s, the Geisels began referring in their letters and holiday cards to an imaginary child named (in Geisel's trademark anapests) "Chrysanthemum-Pearl," a name that combines two traditional symbols of Japan. Geisel's 1938 book *The 500 Hats of Bartholomew Cubbins* included the dedication "To Chrysanthemum-Pearl, aged 89 months, going on 90." Geisel referred to Chrysanthemum-Pearl with such regularity in his correspondence—often bragging about her exploits—that his niece Peggy, among others, believed for years that the Geisels had an actual daughter.

I wanted to thank the extremely helpful librarians at the Dr. Seuss collection at the University of California, San Diego, library for their research assistance on this series.

The Magpies: The magpie is a traditional symbol of Korea. In most European traditions, the magpie is considered a thief and a harbinger of bad luck, while in most East Asian traditions, the magpie brings good news.

Parable of the Magpie in the Trap: The Larsen trap is used to catch magpies by baiting the trap with another living magpie in an inner compartment. Since magpies are highly territorial, they come to attack the decoy bird and are thereby trapped. Larsen traps have been banned as inhumane in much of Europe but are legal in the United Kingdom.

Parable of the Magpie's Name: Pica, an eating disorder which causes people to eat or to crave things that are not food, derives from the Latin name for magpies, who according to folklore would eat anything.

Parable of the Magpie and the Mirror: The mirror test is used to determine whether an animal can recognize itself visually, thus demonstrating self-awareness. The animal's body is marked in an area the animal cannot normally see. The animal is then allowed to view itself in a mirror. If the animal investigates the mark, this demonstrates that it recognizes its own reflection. Very few animals have passed the mirror test: great apes, bottlenose dolphins, Asian elephants, orcas, Eurasian magpies, and ants.

Thirteen Ways of Looking at a Magpie: European folklore tells that magpies steal and hoard shiny objects, a belief popularized by Gioachino Rossini's 1817 opera *La gazza ladra*. However, this myth was disproven by scientists at Exeter University who demonstrated that rather than being attracted to shiny objects, magpies seem to be afraid of them.

Parable of the Magpies in the West: As insect eaters, magpies often land on domestic cattle and sheep to pick off ticks and other insects. This gave rise to the rumor that magpies would burrow into living animals, killing them. Many US states paid bounties for killing magpies, leading to the slaughter of hundreds of thousands of birds—a situation that only ended in 1972, when the Migratory Bird Treaty Act was amended to include magpies.

In the Passive Voice: I began this piece at the Hermitage Artist Retreat in Manasota Key, Florida, and the beach portions of the piece are set there.

Page 121 includes two unattributed quotations: the first is from Seamus Heaney's poem "Station Island," later repeated in "Clearances." The second is from Shel Silverstein's *The Missing Piece*.

Detail of the Rice Chest: This poem is a detail study of the poem "Study of Two Figures (Pasiphaë / Sado)." For information about Crown Prince Sado, please see the notes to the earlier poem. The detail study is in homage to the practice of the late C. D. Wright.

ACKNOWLEDGMENTS

Love and gratitude to the friends who helped me with feedback on this manuscript, often on short notice, including Cathy Park Hong, Claudia Rankine, Mark Thomas Gibson, Meghan O'Rourke, Rick Barot, Stephanie Burt, and Victoria Chang. Thank you to my fellow members of the Racial Imaginary Institute for their deep influence on my thinking about race and artmaking, and a special shout out to Simon Wu for pointing me toward the epigraph for this collection. Thank you to the members of my writers' group, and especially to Nell Freudenberger and Julie Orringer, for offering commiseration, solidarity, and insightful advice. And always endless thanks to the fabulous folks at Graywolf, especially my longtime editor Jeff Shotts, as well as Fiona McCrae and Katie Dublinski, and to Jeenee Lee for her sensitive work on the cover.

My heartfelt thanks to the residencies and retreats at which almost all of this book was written: Civitella Ranieri, the Hermitage Artist Retreat, the Lannan Foundation—Marfa, MacDowell, Vermont Studio Center, and Yaddo. Without the support of these institutions, I simply wouldn't have had the uninterrupted time and headspace necessary to write my poems. Thank you to Princeton and UC Irvine for offering research and travel funding.

Thank you to the editors of the following publications, anthologies, and websites for featuring poems from this collection, sometimes in different versions: The Academy of American Poets' *Poem-A-Day*, *The Adroit Journal*, *The Best American Poetry 2020* (edited by Paisley Rekdal), *The Best American Poetry 2021* (edited by Tracy K. Smith), *BOMB* (print and online), *Harper's Magazine*, *The Nation*, *The New Yorker* (print and online), *The Paris Review*, *Ploughshares*, *Poems for Political Disaster*, *Poetry*, *PBS NewsHour* (online), *The Sewanee Review*, and *The Yale Review*.

Monica Youn grew up in Houston, the daughter of Korean immigrants, and now splits her time between Brooklyn and Southern California, where she is an associate professor of English at UC Irvine. Her previous poetry collections are *Blackacre* (2016), *Ignatz* (2010), and *Barter* (2003). She has been awarded the Levinson Prize from the Poetry Foundation, a Guggenheim Fellowship, the William Carlos Williams Award of the Poetry Society of America, a Witter Bynner Fellowship from the Library of Congress, and a Stegner Fellowship among other honors. She has been a finalist for the National Book Award, the National Book Critics Circle Award, the Kingsley Tufts Award, and the PEN Open Book Award. She is a former constitutional lawyer and a member of the curatorial collective the Racial Imaginary Institute.

The text of *From From* is set in Adobe Garamond Pro.
Book design by Rachel Holscher.
Composition by Bookmobile Design and Digital
Publisher Services, Minneapolis, Minnesota.
Manufactured by Friesens on acid-free,
100 percent postconsumer wastepaper.